1 MONTH OF
FREE
READING

at

www.ForgottenBooks.com

By purchasing this book you are
eligible for one month membership to
ForgottenBooks.com, giving you
unlimited access to our entire
collection of over 1,000,000 titles via
our web site and mobile apps.

To claim your free month visit:

www.forgottenbooks.com/free253388

ISBN 978-0-265-23021-3
PIBN 10253388

PRELIMINARY STUDIES

FOR

A CITY PLAN
FOR OMAHA

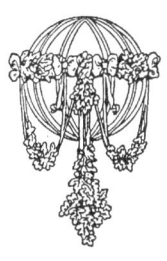

CITY PLANNING COMMISSION
OMAHA, NEBRASKA
NOVEMBER, 1917

CITY PLANNING COMMISSION
OMAHA, NEBRASKA

OFFICERS

GEORGE T. MORTON............_Chairman
B. KVENILD........Secretary and Engineer

OFFICE
THE CITY HALL

MEMBERS

GEORGE B. PRINZ...................1917
EVERETT BUCKINGHAM..............1918
THOMAS A. FRY.,..................1919
J. E. GEORGE.....................1920
GEORGE T. MORTON................1921

*Terms Expiring November 4th of
the Year Given.*

CONSULTING EXPERTS

GEORGE B. FORD   E. P. GOODRICH
CHARLES MULFORD ROBINSON

THE 1915 SESSION LAWS OF NEBRASKA
PROVIDES:

That in each city of the metropolitan class, there shall be a Board known as a City Planning Commission. Said commission shall acquire or prepare a city plan, and shall have power to carry out and maintain said city plan after its adoption by the Mayor and City Council. Said commission shall consist of five members who shall be appointed by the Council, and serve for a term of five years, * * *one member shall be appointed each year. Members of said commission serve without pay. The Mayor and Council shall provide a suitable office for such commission in the City Hall.

TABLE OF CONTENTS

LETTER OF TRANSMISSION

To the Honorable
  Mayor and City Council,

  Omaha, Neb.

Gentlemen:

We take pleasure in submitting a report covering to date the activities of this Commission. For your convenience, we have divided it into two parts.

Part One, covering the twelve months from May, 1916, to May, 1917, was prepared directly by our consulting experts. · It describes the historical development of the city planning idea in Omaha, and the thorough survey of the city and its needs, which was made under their direction. Part Two, based on the showing of Part One, suggests, with the approval of our consultants, an outline of a comprehensive plan for a major street system, for boulevard additions and corrections, and the Commission's recommendations for the elimination of grade crossings along the Belt Line Railway.

We would emphasize the preliminary and tentative character of these suggestions. Much earnest study has been given to them. We believe that they are practical, and that for the most part, they can be carried through at comparatively little cost. We are confident that in their gradual realization the city would gain greatly. At the same time, we would emphasize the fact that no comprehensive city plan, looking far into the future for complete accomplishment, can be final. In a growing city, new conditions must constantly arise, and it is impossible to forsee all the changes which the years will bring. We do not contend then, that the plan outlined in the following pages is complete in all details, for there have been scant funds and little time for that, nor do we suggest that any portion of it, once accepted, can be never changed. Our purpose, in common with all city plan commissions, has been rather to substitute the community viewpoint for the individuals; the long view for the short view; to think of the greater Omaha of tomorrow instead of the Omaha of today, and of the benefit to the city at large rather than of the gain to private land owners. If the spirit and general principles of our suggestions are approved, and the city so desires, we hold ourselves in readiness to prepare more detailed studies of such improvements as the Council may request. Meanwhile and always, we shall welcome the comments and suggestions of the public.

Many other problems of a city planning character press for solution besides those herein considered. The outside boulevard system is barely touched upon; the treatment of the City's wonderful ravines cries out for study; new parks and playgrounds, the location of rapid transit lines, the development of waterfront facilities, railroad terminals, industrial housing, and the reasonable control over private property in the interest of the community as a whole—all these matters which must be considered in the plans for a more efficient and more beautiful Omaha, for a city better to live in, and better to work in. We have made only a beginning, but we believe it is a long and important start, and if what has been accomplished with limited funds, and in limited time, commends itself to the public and your honorable body, we shall be glad of authority and opportunity to carry our work farther.

A complete map has been prepared of the city and its surrounding territory, as of 1917, filling a greatly felt want. We have also, at the request of the Board of Education, prepared a map, based on this, showing the school districts of greater Omaha, and for the Election Commissioner, a ward map of the greater city. To the Superintendent of Public Improvements, Mr. W. S. Jardine, and to the City Engineer, Mr. John A. Bruce, we make our grateful acknowledgments for sympathetic support and services. We recognize also the interest of Mr. Joseph B. Hummel, Superintendent of Parks and Public Property, in that important portion of our work which concerns his department.

Respectfully submitted,

GEORGE T. MORTON,
GEORGE B. PRINZ,
EVERETT BUCKINGHAM,
THOMAS A. FRY,
J. E. GEORGE,

Members of City Planning Commission.

B. KVENILD,
Secretary and Engineer.

November, 1917.

PART ONE

PREPARATION

Report of the First Year
May 1916, May 1917

BEGINNINGS

On May 15, 1916, the City Planning Commission, which had been appointed a few months earlier, opened offices in the City Hall, retained B. Kvenild, of Omaha as its Secretary, and engaged Messrs. George B. Ford, Ernest P. Goodrich and Charles Mulford Robinson as its consulting experts. The two first named are of New York City, and the latter is of Rochester, New York. On that date, then, positive work on a city plan for Omaha actually began.

It would be interesting, and doubtless instructive, to rehearse the long, slow processes of agitation, education and finally legislation; which had gained for Omaha the right to have a City Planning Commission; but those operations extend over a long period. Suffice to say here that in November of 1915, the following gentlemen were appointed by the Mayor and City Council to serve as the City Planning Commissioners of Omaha: George Brandeis, Everett Buckingham, Thomas A. Fry, George T. Morton and George B. Prinz; all men of prominence, highly respected in the community, having behind them a record of success in their private affairs. In November, 1916, Mr. Brandeis resigned and J. E. George was appointed to take his place, an appointment which has fully sustained the high standard of the commission's personnel.

The Commission promptly organized by electing Mr. Morton as Chairman, and requested the City Council for an appropriation. Early in the new year the Council set aside the sum of $7,500.00 for the Commission's use during 1916. While this was a small sum with which to begin so large a task, it was all available for the work in hand, the Commissioners themselves serving without pay, and their office in the City Hall being given them rent free. In fact, even the furnishings of the office were kept down to the bare necessities of efficient operation; a conference table and two draughting boards comprising the principle articles.

Much care, involving considerable correspondence, was exercised in the choice of the secretary and of the experts, on whom would fall the technical work of preparing the city plan. Once the choice was made and the contracts entered into, the active planning for the future of Omaha may be said to have gotten under way. In Omaha, Mr. Kvenild was in frequent conference with the Commissioners; both the chairman and the secretary entered into close correspondence with the experts, and in New York the latter three prepared in conference, a program for the year's operations, outlining in detail the various steps of the comprehensive study to be undertaken.

THE SURVEY

Few laymen realize the thoroughness with which the science of city planning is now taken up. This study, once entered upon in a light-hearted fashion, bases its recommendations today on investigations at once so comprehensive and detailed, that no city is able to furnish from its records, all the data which is desired. It is realized that the city of the future must so clearly grow out of the city of the present, that the first essential step is to know all the present conditions. Those conditions are not engineering feats alone. The time has gone when the city planner can be just a municipal engineer. He must be also an efficiency engineer and sociologist.

That fact explains why the City Planning Commission of Omaha selected three consultants instead of one—because no one man can know so much on so many different subjects as Omaha wants its experts to know. The choice, accordingly, was made of three men who had specialized along distinctive lines. Mr. Ford is an architect who has had particular experience in the districting of cities; Mr. Goodrich is an engineer who has had particular experience in the problems of transportation, while Mr. Robinson has specialized on street and park planning.

FIRST SPECIFIC PROBLEMS

Hardly had the experts and secretary been selected, when the pressing problem of separating the railroad grade crossings where Dodge, Douglas and Farnam Streets cross the

Missouri Pacific Belt Line, called Mr. Goodrich to Omaha. In early June, Chairman Morton, Secretary Kvenild, and the three consultants, made the convention in Cleveland of the National Conference of City Planning the occasion for a meeting; and a month later the consultants paid a joint visit to Omaha for personal investigation, study and conferences. At this time, the study of the grade crossing problem, participated in by Secretary Kvenild, the three experts, City Engineer Bruce and the railroad engineers was completed, and a careful report recommending elevation of the tracks and giving the details of that operation, was submitted to the Council. This report not only included technical data as to the construction and design, but detailed estimates of cost, enabling the Council to act on complete information.

During this visit also, Messrs. Ford, Goodrich and Robinson examined all parts of the city, took many notes and photographs, conferred with officials and other citizens, and gave consideration to a number of other specific problems.

Of more importance, however, than even these specific studies—taking the long view—were the conferences held with City Attorney Rine for the purpose of ascertaining just what new legislation would be needed to facilitate the carrying out of the City Plan, and to promote the city's most efficient development, conferences which shortly led to the preparation and discussion of definite bills. Most important, also, was the comprehensive grasp which the consultants gained of Omaha's many sided city planning problem, and the series of "surveys," or data-maps, of which they authorized and directed the preparation. To assist in the latter, Mr. Robinson and Mr. Ford returned to Omaha from time to time. It is believed that from a graphic standpoint these maps represent the most practical and workman-like survey preliminary to a city plan ever made for an American City.

DATA MAPS

There are eighteen of the maps, the experts acknowledging their indebtedness to Mr. Kvenild and his draughtsman for the careful work that went into them. The maps, all drawn to the same scale, show:

1. USE OF LAND: This indicates the varying uses to which the building area within the city limits has been put,

different conventions indicating business property, industrial, residential, municipal, state and county, and railroad lands. Such a map may be considered as providing the fundamental groundwork for a city plan, of which the purpose is to fit each portion of the city in the best possible way for the work it has to do. The map reveals how business, spreading beyond the "down-town" section, has already advanced along the lines of least resistance and heaviest travel—as south on Thirteenth and Sixteenth Streets, west on Leavenworth, Farnam and Cuming, north on Twenty-fourth above Cuming, avoiding in each case, streets of heavy grade. It shows where the subsidiary business centers are developing—not only on an important scale around the packing houses in South Omaha, but as neighborhood centers at selected street intersections—sometimes, in their uncontrolled wilfulness, to the great detriment of adjoining residential property—and, again, as advance outposts far along the routes on which, nearer the city's center, business is progressing on its outward march—so showing clearly that the march is to continue, and that the street should be prepared for its conquest by business. This map will, therefore, be of great value in suggesting the city's future requirements.

2. THE LOCATION OF THE WORKING POPULATION: Here are shown the places at which the wage earners work, (building trades and domestic service being omitted). Each dot represents fifty people. The map well supplements Number 1, for it not only shows where the industrial establishments are, but the number of their employees. Very striking is its depiction of the relatively high proportion employed by the railroads and stock yards, the spreading of industry out Izard Street—these conditions partly explaining the advance of business upon Cuming and Izard, and accounting for the development of the important business center in South Omaha. For where men daily go and where they receive their wages, business gathers.

3. THE DISTRIBUTION OF POPULATION: The purpose of this map is to show where the people live, the same numerical unit—fifty people to a dot—having been adopted as on the map last described. It is most interesting to study the three maps side by side, observing how one grows out of another; how inevitable are the laws of urban development; but there is more than that to the present map. At

a glance one sees where are the congested blocks, where the city planner must be on the watch for over-crowding, for tenements, and for bad housing conditions generally; where the need is sorest for playgrounds and open spaces; and where, on the other hand, the street provision is in excess of the probable requirements of the population for years to come.

· 4. THE LOCATION OF AREAS WHERE DWELLINGS ARE CROWDED OR UNSANITARY: Because housing conditions are of far reaching importance to the community, they have been made the subject of a special map, supplementing Number 3. On this map cross hatching shows the unsanitary houses, and the solid black the houses located on the rear of lots. Both are much too numerous for a city in which the average density of population is as light as in Omaha. For this, the long lots and the general adoption of an alley system are in large part responsible. The condition is one which is dangerous to the welfare of the community.

5. EXISTING AND PROPOSED SEWERS: Reassuring, after the last map, is the showing of the extent to which Omaha is provided with sewers—though some strange gaps still remain, and a good many sewers have yet to be constructed, in South Omaha particularly. It appears that generally sewers exist in the areas of unsanitary housing. Consequently, the perfectly reasonable requirement of connection with them may be expected to affect a large improvement, without further cost to the community.

6. PARKS, PLAYGROUNDS AND SCHOOL PROPERTY: Greatly enhancing not only the interest, but the value, of this map, are the circles which have been drawn around each park and playground as a center. These circles have radii of one-quarter and one-half mile, the former showing the maximum distance which small children can be expected to walk to a playground, and the latter the distance from which older children and adults will walk to a park or playground. These circles, therefore, define the area of service by Omaha's parks and playgrounds. Well provided as the city appears to be with recreation areas, it is surprising to observe how considerable in extent and in importance, are the sections which, outside any circles, are not served directly by park or playground—for which, indeed, no such spaces have been provided. There are other areas within the circles, which

are not served adequately because the parks or playgrounds have not yet been fully developed. ·

7. LOCATION OF THE SCHOOL POPULATION: On this map are shown the boundaries of each school district, the location of its school house, the amount of ground the property includes, and the number of children whom it attempts to serve, each dot representing twenty-five school children. It offers an interesting supplement to the Park and Playground map, for now one can see not only what areas are not within practicable reach of a recreation ground, but just how many children are deprived of such essential facilities.

8. PLACES WHERE FOODSTUFFS ARE SOLD: Markets of all kinds are here shown, the wholesale and retail being differentiated by conventional signs. In this map there is material for a local study of some aspects of that pressing question—the high cost of living. It was included among the city planning data maps because the city efficient, convenient and economical, is the goal of the city planners. For a like reason, there has been drawn—

9. A TRANSIT MAP: This not only gives all the car lines, but indicates where they are single and where double track, and the location of the transfer points. Then timelines have been drawn to show what parts of the city can be reached in a five-minute, ten-minute, fifteen-minute, twenty-minute, twenty-five-minute, and half-hour trip from the city's center. The irregularity of these time lines offer striking proof of how excellently served some portions of Omaha are, and how still deficient in transportation facilities some other portions are—one section for instance, which is only a mile and a half from the city's center, being as far from it in time as are other sections three miles from the center. It is interesting, however, and encouraging to note that nearly all the area of the city, barring a fringe on the southern and northern edges, can be reached in a ride of not over thirty minutes.

10. CONTOURS AND STREET GRADIENTS: This is probably one of the most remarkable city maps ever drawn. There are other cities which have contours as difficult and streets that are even steeper than Omaha's, but their conditions are yet to be graphically presented. On this map, street grades of less than five per cent are white, five to ten per cent are black, and grades above ten per cent are dotted.

Even with the fortunate ease with which cuts and fills can be made in the rockless earth of Omaha, and notwithstanding the stupendous scale on which they have been made, the white streets are wonderfully few. Most interesting, also, is the showing by the contour lines that diagonal thoroughfares, running northwest from the business center, might have been laid out at an almost even grade to Fort Omaha and Miller Park; but the rectangular street plan adopted at the beginning, where the ground was comparatively level, has been rigidly adhered to from end to end of the city limits, regardless of topography, or of costs exacted in construction, in energy and in time. Beyond the western limits, and therefore not shown on the map, modern ideas in planning have been followed, and there the newer parts of the growing city are coming into their own, in the beauty which nature put in Omaha's grasp.

11. TRUCKING AND AUTOMOBILE ROUTES: Fully to appreciate this map's significance, one must study it with the map showing contours and street grades. Only then can one realize the extent of the economic tax which is put upon all kinds of business in Omaha by the heavy grades. The tax is increased by another circumstance, which the map shows clearly. This is the remarkable lack of streets which go through without a break—usually the one great merit of a standardized street plan. In Omaha there are probably not six long streets which are continuous from end to end, and uniform. Even Twenty-fourth, which is generally thought of as a through street, has several jogs and varies in width. West of Twenty-fourth there is absolutely no through north and south street, and the city limits are more than two miles beyond Twenty-fourth. Here certainly is a challenging problem for the city planners.

12. EXISTING PAVEMENTS: Omaha is on the whole, a pretty well paved city. With the city's steep grades, macadam would so soon wash out that it has been necessary to lay a great deal of hard pavement. For this purpose brick and concrete have been especially utilized, although nearly every kind of pavements may be found as the map indicates. It is most interesting to check up this map with those showing the street grades, and the popular automobile and truck routes.

13. CUSTOMARY AND POSSIBLE PARKING PLACES FOR AUTOMOBILES: The feature of this map is the remarkable extent of the parking facilities in the business district. Thanks to the pioneer city planners who first laid out the streets of that district, and gave them a generous width, Omaha has been relieved, to a considerable extent, of one of the most serious and baffling of the modern problems of city planning.

14. POSSIBLE CONNECTIONS BETWEEN DEAD ENDS OF STREETS AND POSSIBLE WIDENINGS: This map constitutes a preliminary study of the problem offered by the conditions shown in Map Eleven. When it is seen how urgent improvement is in order that Omaha may gain a system of through and adequate thoroughfares, and when it is realized that each possibility must be studied in detail, there will be appreciation of how great a task the city planning of Omaha is, and how extended and continuous a process it must be, if it is to do for Omaha all that it can do. Fortunately, it will be possible to affect a great number of these improvements at little or no expense to the community at large.

15. RAILROAD PROPERTY AND LOCATION AND CHARACTER OF RAILROAD STREET CROSSINGS: The importance of Omaha as a railroad terminal needs no better proof than a glance at this map will offer. Great railroad systems stand behind the city's commercial future; but the very extent of the investments which they have made in Omaha lands, complicates and adds to the difficulties of the local planning problem. The special data map devoted to this subject and showing not only the railroad-owned property, but the character of every crossing of street and railroad, was required by the experts because of their recognition of the extent and seriousness of these problems. The ideal of the city planners is not the city throttled, but the city built up by railroads.

16. THE DISTRIBUTION OF PROPERTY VALUES: On this map black lines divide the city into areas of all sorts of shapes and sizes, the areas being determined by the lands having a like value per front foot. What these values are, approximately, is shown by the figures that are framed in the district lines. While for full understanding this map must be carefully studied in connection with the data already described, there is much of interest to be read in the map even when taken alone. Very significant, for instance, is the

sudden rise of values when one reaches the Happy Hollow district, with the property restrictions and its modernly planned streets; the drop in values which is caused by the proximity of railroads; the development of high values far out on streets which other data have shown to be destined to traffic and business importance; the upward spurt in values on lands adjacent to parks; the quick drop where local transportation facilities are poor; and the very considerable amount of close-in property which, of generous depth, can still be bought for about $10.00 a front foot. In a city as large as Omaha, this latter is most encouraging, for even after making allowances for topographical difficulties, the condition holds out the promise of a solution of the housing problem. As in all the data maps, so in this one particularly, the more one studies it the more one sees.

17. STREET LIGHTING MAP: Here are shown the location of the street lights of Omaha, with indications of whether they are electric or gas. The persistence of gas through the middle zone, the streets for which special illumination has been provided, the inadequate lighting of portions of the boulevards, the occasional dark areas in a city of light—all this is interestingly and suggestively laid bare.

18. PUBLIC AND SEMI-PUBLIC BUILDINGS: Churches and other places of worship, schools of all kinds, charitable institutions of every sort, fire stations and public buildings, the units of each group having their own distinguishing mark, are located on this map. Embryo neighborhood centers are revealed; the location and extent of areas insufficiently provided with structures of a public or semi-public character; and yet, and most striking of all, the great aggregate of such buildings in a progressive modern city, are among the revelations of the map.

No one can go over this collection of data maps without a strong impression of the worth-whileness of the work, or without feeling an increased assurance as to the value of plans and recommendations based on a study at once so comprehensive and so thorough. Few cities in the world, perhaps not any in the United States, have had their present conditions so clearly charted as a foundation for a city plan. Omaha may now know itself, and can think of itself in a big way, realizing that in city planning the whole community, not a neighborhood, not a clique, not one street or one interest, or one department of the city government, is the unit. The city plan is as inclusive as the city.

THE EXHIBITION

Recognizing the educational value of the data thus secured and tabulated in graphic form, the City Planning Commission, on recommendation of the consultants, arranged late in 1916 a public exhibition. Space was kindly given for this in the corridors of the Court House—a central location—and the exhibition, open from December 13th to December 31st, inclusive, was visited by thousands of people. The data maps were supplemented by enlargements of many of the photographs taken by the experts, and with exhibits furnished by other departments of the city. This section of the exhibit offered a complete view not only of the Omaha of today, but of the current preparations for the Omaha of tomorrow.

In addition, there were two other sections. One comprised a large collection of well prepared city planning material which had been obtained from the American City Bureau. This was classified according to the subject—as transit, playgrounds, etc., and John E. Lathrop of the Bureau was in constant attendance, explaining the exhibit. During his visit, he also aroused wide public interest by his addresses to clubs and societies throughout the city. A third section, furnished by the consultants, showed city planning material arranged according to cities, these screens offering a striking view of the progress which other municipalities are making.

Clearly, in the preparation of the series of data maps and in the carrying on of the exhibition, the year 1916 saw a great deal accomplished.

PLANNING FOR 1917

At the Commission's request, the experts gave much thought and time to the preparation of a 1917 program which could be based on the broad foundation thus securely laid. The extent and comprehensiveness of the outline will be appreciated when it is said that twenty-two distinct groups of subjects were included. But, unfortunately for the Commission's hopes, the appropriation by the City Council for 1917 failed by sixty per cent to meet the budget so carefully prepared. The seriousness of the reduction was in reality greater even than appears, for with certain fixed charges, such as the salaries of secretary and draughtsmen—to be taken out, the Commission found its margin for forward work reduced by about seventy-five per cent. A radical revision of program was, therefore, necessitated.

After earnest consideration, it was then decided to take up in particular, for 1917, three lines of activity, viz., zoning or districting; the extension, widening and regrading of main traffic streets; and the study of scenic drives and public reservations, postponing until later, the many other important phases of a city plan.

Taking up districting first, because in the view both of the consultants and Commission, this promised particular benefits to all the people of the city, maps were prepared to show: (a) the present use of property—whether for residence, industry or trade; (b) the heights of existing buildings; (c) the percentage of lot area covered by buildings; and (d) the character and material of existing buildings. Meanwhile, the city attorney in consultation with the advisers of the Commission, prepared an enabling bill to permit the city to form the districts which might be proposed in the plan. This bill passed the lower house and up to final vote in the senate. No opposition appearing against the bill, its passage seemed assured. However, on the last day of the session of the Senate, it unexpectedly failed to pass in the rush of final consideration of the many bills. Happily, the data contained on the maps will be serviceable in other work for Omaha, and with little modification, will be again available for districting studies when that fundamental city planning operation shall at last be authorized.

We did get legislation extending the city's control of the platting of new additions three miles outside the city limits; the right to grade several intersecting streets in one grading district where a majority petition for it; and some additional power, but not sufficient, to open or widen streets. The old limitation of $50,000 maximum cost of any such improvement that may be carried out by the Council, was raised to $100,000, in cases where the Planning Commission recommend it, and the special benefit tax may be paid in five annual installments, instead of all in one payment.

In all the work at the Legislature, we must acknowledge the hearty support of business and civic organizations, even though some of them would be directly restricted by these laws. The Commercial Club, Real Estate Board, Building Owners' and Managers' Association, Improvement Clubs, the press, and the public generally worked with us unselfishly.

The Commission and its consultants now turned to the other features of the program—the platting of a major street system and of scenic drives and reservations.

An idea of the speed and thoroughness with which this work was now pushed, is afforded by a glance at the maps which relate to it. For the traffic studies there were under way by May maps showing street widths, roadway widths, age of pavements, ungraded streets, building setbacks, the location of street trees, and traffic counts. For the scenic drives, tentative routes were laid out, after careful consideration of grades and views. For the reservations, areas are being designated for acquisition as viewpoints, outlooks, parks and playgrounds, and for the preservation of natural scenery. The purpose is to insure to all the people of Omaha, and to its visitors, the enjoyment of some of the natural beauty with which the city is endowed.

THE WAR

The Commission does not forget in all its work, nor do its consultants, that the Nation has entered into war. Inquiry has been made as to the attitude of Commissions in other cities and even abroad. It is found that, as a consequence of war, city planning everywhere is regarded as an even more vital and pressing subject than before. Stricken France is actually taking up today on a great scale, the planning and re-planning of her cities, because she has learned that in municipal, as in other affairs, economy and the prevention of waste can be secured only by planning. In Omaha, in this time of national crisis, there is no more urgent need than the prevention of waste in the movement of the people, in the handling and movement of goods, and in the development and use of land. With this thought in mind, earnest study has proceeded for the provision of the best practicable traffic ways.

As the Commission said, in closing its report to the Council at the end of 1916:

"Omaha is rapidly becoming one of the great metropolitan cities of the country. Population statistics show that within thirty years, it will have a population of at least half a million. The city must be prepared to meet this growth with an adequate system of thoroughfares and transit lines; with generous railroad and water front facilities; with adequate and well distributed places for recreation, and with reasonable control over private property in the interest of the community as a whole. Your various departments are doing excellent work, each in their respective line, but the problems are multiplying rapidly and becoming constantly more complex and interdependent. Omaha can no longer afford to fritter away its energy on petty details. It is ready to face the big things. It is no longer a child; it is ready to look at things with a man's point of view."

GEORGE B. FORD,
E. P. GOODRICH,
CHAS. MULFORD ROBINSON.

PART TWO

RECOMMENDATIONS
AND SUGGESTIONS

Elimination of Grade Crossing on the Belt Line Railway

The City Planning Commission has studied at considerable length, all of the questions involved in the elimination of the railroad grade crossings of the major streets by the Omaha Belt Line. In our communication to the City Council of July 18, 1916, we recommended the elevation of the tracks from Dodge Street to Farnam Street, as the plan most advantageous to the city and to the adjacent property. In adopting this scheme, the city practically settled upon the course to follow in eliminating the balance of the grade crossings. The topography of the country, the need of the industries and yards along the Belt Line, and the operating needs of the Railroad Company, further indicate this.

The Railroad Company's aim must be to flatten the grades in order to insure more economic operation. This will benefit the patrons and the city will be the gainer, as the improvement will be the means of doing away with some of the noise and heavy smoke.

The following fundamental considerations have dictated our solution of the problem: *The development of the plan for improvement should be laid out in such a manner that it can be executed progressively, at a reasonable cost, to the best advantage of the abutting property owners, and to the city as a whole.*

Our drawing No. 1, showing the present and proposed top of rail of the Belt Line, shows that it is proposed to elevate the tracks from 16th Street to Ruggles Street; to elevate them from Cuming Street to the present elevation at Dodge Street, and to elevate them from Farnam Street to a point south of Pacific Street on the South Omaha branch line. The main line will be elevated from Dewey Avenue to the south of Center Street. The Railroad Company will probably, of its own accord, make a cut at Center Street on the South Omaha connection, and at Hamilton Street, extending in each case north and south to meet the proposed elevation. This improvement does not enter into our grade crossing elimination plan, because the major streets there already are separated from the railroad.

In proposing the elimination of only a few grade crossings, we do not contend that the intermediate crossings should **not** be eliminated. Our contention is that after the major street crossings are abolished, it is merely a local affair to do away with others as the need arises in the various locations.

We wish to caution against closing or vacating any street now crossing the Belt Line until a complete study of the street system has been made. The time might come when the street will be wanted and when an elimination of grade crossing at that point will be urgently needed.

Under the plan, the railroad grade crossings of the following major streets, are to be eliminated:

1. Commecial Avenue,
2. Florence Boulevard,
3. Twenty-fourth Street,
4. Twenty-seventh Street,
5. Thirtieth Street,
6. Sprague Street,
7. Bedford Avenue,
8. Thirty-sixth Street,
9. Lake Street,
10. Fortieth Street,
11. Saddle Creek Road leading northwest,
12. California Street,
13. Dewey Avenue,
14. Saddle Creek Road leading southwest,
15. Forty-second Street,
16. Leavenworth Street,
17. Pacific Street,
18. Arbor Street,
19. Vinton Street.

On the main line from Dewey Avenue south:

1. Leavenworth Street,
2. Forty-eighth Street,
3. Pacific Street,
4. Fifty-second Street,
5. Center Street,
6. Sixtieth Street,
7. Boulevard connection between Hanscom Park and Elmwood Park.

The elimination of the grade crossings at Lake and Fortieth Streets may not be required for many years. When the times does come that Lake Street and Fortieth Street have developed into efficient east-west and north-south major streets, a separation of grade may be deemed advisable in spite of the heavy expense caused by property damage.

At present, the topography of this section of the city, and the fact that both Lake Street and Fortieth Street are merely local traffic streets, make it almost more desirable to maintain the grade crossings than to eliminate them.

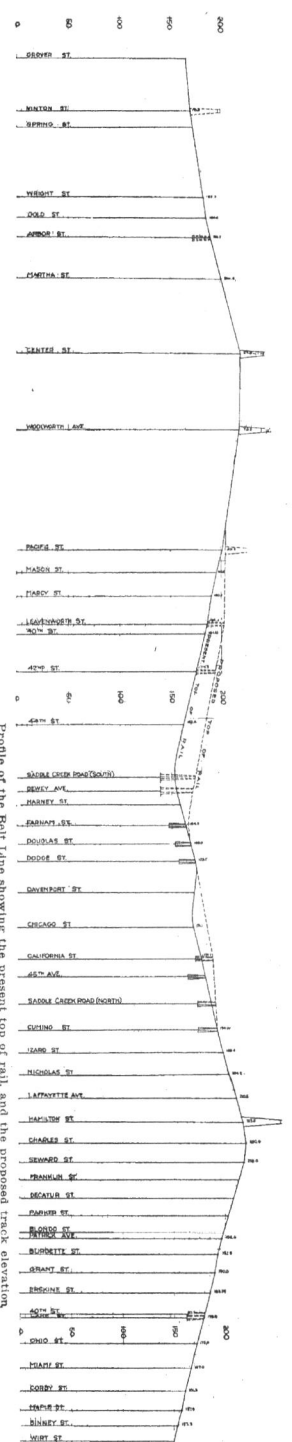

Profile of the Belt Line showing the present top of rail, and the proposed track elevation.

The elimination of the grade crossings at Lake and Fortieth Streets may not be required for many years. When the times does come that Lake Street and Fortieth Street have developed into efficient east-west and north-south major streets, a separation of grade may be deemed advisable in spite of the heavy expense caused by property damage.

At present, the topography of this section of the city, and the fact that both Lake Street and Fortieth Street are merely local traffic streets, make it almost more desirable to maintain the grade crossings than to eliminate them.

Boulevards and Drives

It may be said that the dignity and beauty of a city depends, to a large extent, on its boulevards and scenic drives. Yet, it cannot be expected that Omaha can afford a comprehensive boulevard system unless it pursues a steady and continous policy in acquiring and developing them.

Omaha with a population of 215,000 now has a park area of approximately 991 acres, and a boulevard system 35 miles long. The boulevards, however, are lacking in continuity at various places, and in particular afford no connection between Hanscom Park and Elmwood Park. To remedy these conditions, the following suggestions are offered:

1. A connection between Hanscom Park and Elmwood Park by extending Woolworth Avenue through the County Poor Farm, and thence in a southwesterly direction to the intersection of Forty-fifth Street and Center Street, as previously has been suggested by the Superintendent of Parks and Boulevards. From this point, it is suggested that Center Street constitute the boulevard to a point where it crosses the Missouri Pacific tracks. Thence the boulevard would follow Saddle Creek in a southwesterly direction to the junction between the Missouri Pacific Railroad and the Chicago & Northwestern Railroad. There it would turn northwestward, crossing the Missouri Pacific Railway, and follow the Little Papillion to its intersection with the Happy Hollow Creek. Thence it would proceed northeasterly to Elmwood Park. Where Center Street is used from Forty-fifth Street to the crossing of the Missouri Pacific, a widening should be affected, this widening to include the creek bed along the street which now is useless for anything but boulevard property. Attention is called to the fact that the property which it is proposed to acquire along the various creeks for the construction of the boulevard, will at some later time, be needed by the Engineering Department for the construction of sewers. It is the opinion of the Planning Commission, that a boulevard route proposed above, using part of the way one of the principal streets leading to the city, and farther out, located in a beautiful valley, and in other places passing through the wooded lands along the picturesque creeks, would be an admirable boulevard link, and useful

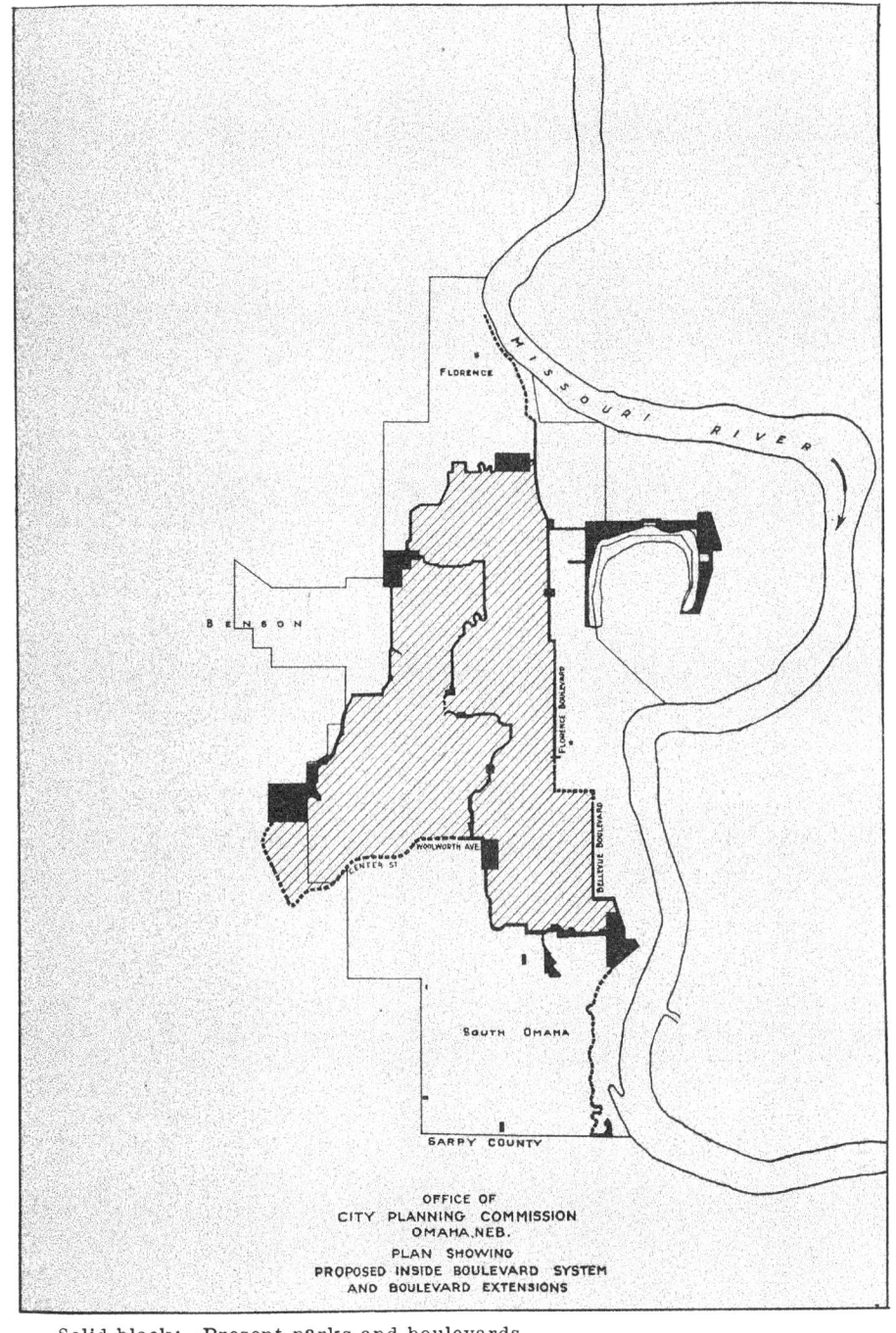

Solid black:—Present parks and boulevards.
Dotted black:—Proposed extensions.
Cross-hatched area:—Part of the city fairly well equipped with boulevards
when extensions are completed.

to the city as a whole, because its construction will be inexpensive, and its route logical. This route also has the advantage of preceding the development of the district. A shorter connection between Hanscom Park and Elmwood Park has been suggested, but not enough study has been given such a route to determine its feasibility.

2. A distinct boulevard connection to be made between Bemis Park and the beginning of John A. Creighton Boulevard at Hamilton Street by means of Thirty-eighth Street. As it is now, Creighton Boulevard, with its many possibilities, is very little used, to the detriment of the property along it. Consequently, it is an expense to the city without bringing adequate returns.

3. Florence Boulevard at its termination at Chicago Street to be continued south on Nineteenth Street to Jackson Street at such time as the Dodge Street hill is cut; then east on Jackson Street to its intersection with Bellevue Boulevard, thus connecting two separate boulevards and avoiding the confusion in pleasure traveling through the central part of the city. The parts of Jackson Street and Nineteenth Street mentioned above do not necessarily need to be declared a boulevard with accompanying restrictions. The Commission's idea is only that there be boulevard features such as special ornamental lights, or other distinctive features, to indicate that it is a boulevard connection.

4. The intersection of Bellevue Boulevard (Eleventh Street) and Bancroft Street to be made safe and more dignified by acquiring additional property on the northeast corner.

5. Thirty-second Avenue from Woolworth Avenue to Ed. Creighton Avenue and Ed. Creighton Avenue from Thirty-second Avenue to Hanscom Boulevard, are now extensively used as a boulevard connection in preference to Hanscom Park, with its steep grades and sharp curves. The use of this connection ought to be facilitated by correcting the southwest corner of Hanscom Park, where Ed. Creighton Avenue intersects Thirty-second Avenue, and the southwest corner of Hanscom Boulevard and Ed. Creighton Avenue.

The improvements and new construction mentioned above will, together with the present boulevards, give the city a complete inside boulevard system as shown on our map.

In addition to these improvements, considerable time has been spent by the Commission in the study of an extension of Florence Boulevard north, and of a boulevard extending from Dorcas Street and Tenth Street south to Child's Point. In themselves, these are independent boulevards, yet they are a part of a future comprehensive outside boulevard system, and we submit the following notes on them:

EXTENSION OF FLORENCE BOULEVARD

Florence Boulevard ends now rather abruptly on the north at Read Street. An extension would be possible in a northwesterly direction on the low lands west of the Chicago & Northwestern Railroad, crossing under the railroad at Scott Street. The present railroad bridge at this point should be rebuilt when the boulevard is constructed. From this point the boulevard would run in a northeasterly direction until it intersects the abandoned Chicago & Northwestern track, and thence along the abandoned track through the Metropolitan Water District's property, where an admirable boulevard drive already is a reality, connecting with the River Road to Blair, north of the Pumping Station.

THIRTEENTH STREET BOULEVARD

One of the most interesting scenic views of Omaha is to be found in the slopes on the west side of the Missouri River, extending from Dorcas Street south to Child's Point. At almost any point along this stretch, (which is approximately four miles in length,) one views fertile farm land, a wide, interesting river in which the sky, the hills, and the distance are reflected, and around it all is the sky line of distant forest clad hillsides. Nature has not made these slopes suitable for farming, but has made them beautiful, and most of them still are covered with forest. Since this land has little commercial value, it could be acquired at slight cost, and should be preserved in a state of nature. Such a preservation would have scientific value, both in respect to forestry and to wild life. But, above all, it would have priceless value for those who live in or visit Omaha. Within half an hour they could pass from the bustle of the city to the seclusion of the forest.

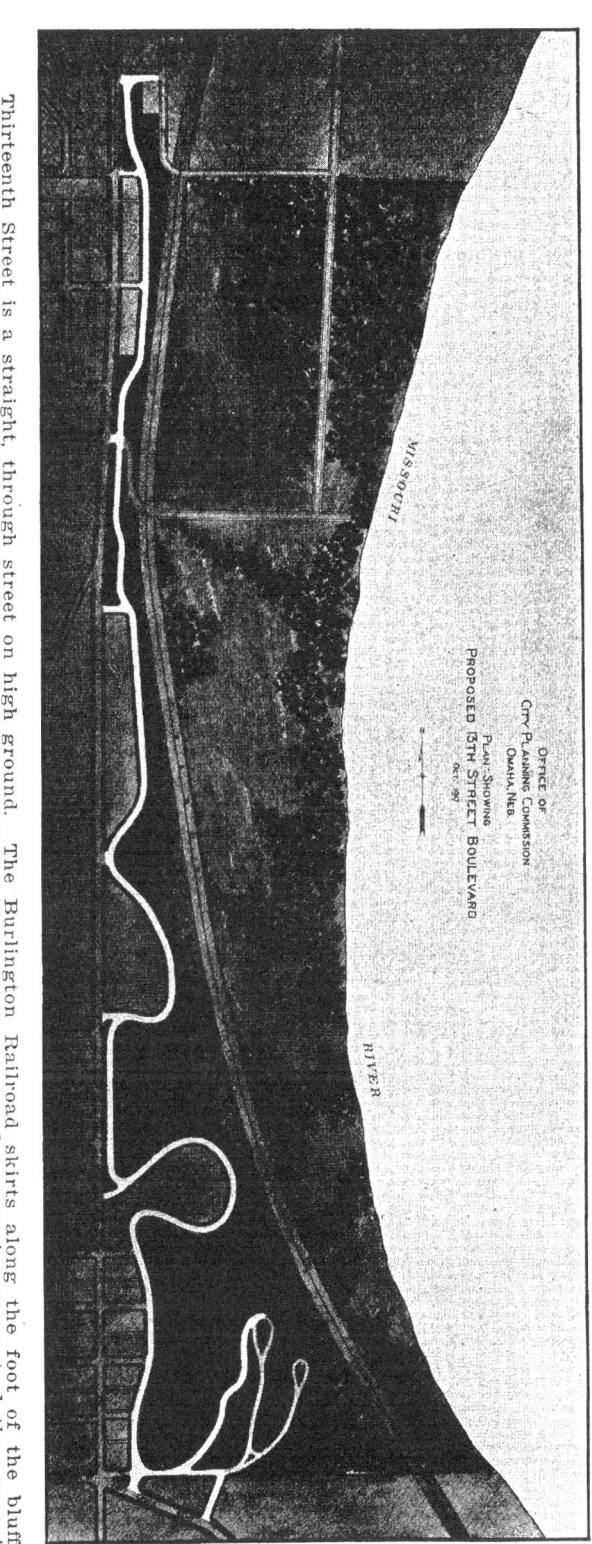

OFFICE OF
City Planning Commission
Omaha, Neb.
Plan Showing
Proposed 13th Street Boulevard
Oct. 1917

MISSOURI

RIVER

Thirteenth Street is a straight, through street on high ground. The Burlington Railroad skirts along the foot of the bluff 50 to 100 feet below. The proposed drive, in white, skirts the top of the bluff. It is proposed to acquire or control the present waste bluff and bottom land east of this drive. Thirteenth Street will continue to carry the through traffic, and will from several points, command beautiful views of the park area and river, and the Iowa shore. The winding park drive will be for the slower travel of those wishing to more leisurely admire the wonderful beauties of nature displayed here.

View of the pleasing landscape, the proposed Thirteenth Street Boulevard will overlook just north of "Q" Street. The bottom land and bluff will be left with its present wild growth, and the drive will be at the top of the bluff.

The route mentioned above may be divided into four distinct parts, as follows:

From Dorcas Street to Riverview Park,
From Riverview Park to J Street,
From J Street to Mandan Park,
From Mandan Park to Child's Point.

DORCAS STREET TO RIVERVIEW PARK

The route for the drive from Dorcas Street to Riverview Park has been studied and a map has been prepared showing its approximate location, but the need of more intensive studies prohibits a definite recommendation in this report.

RIVERVIEW PARK TO J STREET

The Superintendent of Parks and Boulevards has made a survey of a proposed drive from Riverview Park to J Street. This section in itself would hardly be worth while unless it constitutes a part of continuous drive from Riverview Park to Mandan Park. As such, it is well located, and will be an admirable part of the South River Drive.

J STREET TO MANDAN PARK

The route from J Street to Mandan Park has been studied carefully by the Commission. The absence of contour maps east of Thirteenth Street has made it impossible to establish a definite location, but enough information is on hand to recommend an approximate location. The City Planning Commission recommends that sufficient land be acquired from J Street to Mandan Park, to construct a drive approximating the accompanying plan. It is further recommended that enough land be acquired to protect such drives and preserve the view and their usefulness for all time to come. To obtain this object, it will be necessary to acquire or control all land from the proposed drive east to the river, and from Missouri Avenue south to the city limits, except the railroad right-of-way.

In connection with acquiring this property, it is suggested that steps be taken to acquire or control the island in the Missouri River south of Riverview Park, as a bird reserve for all time to come. The boulevard property, the Island

and the Audubon Society's Reserve on Child's Point, which has been promoted by the Fontenelle Forest Association, will then be of national importance as a resting and nesting place for the migrating and domestic birds. Properly developed, this whole South River Drive will be a strikingly attractive feature of Omaha's development, far surpassing in scenic interest, the famous Cliff Drive of Kansas City.

MANDAN PARK TO CHILD'S POINT

The route from Mandan Park to Child's Point is outside Douglas County, and will not be discussed in this report except to suggest better connections between the proposed drive and the Fort Crook Boulevard at points where the loop entering the park joins Harrison Street. By widening an existing alley for half a block, the southwest corner of the park may be connected to the Fort Crook Boulevard, by cutting off the sharp corner at Thirteenth Street, and Harrison Street, a direct connection is provided from the River Drive to Fort Crook Boulevard, for travel not wishing to detour through the park.

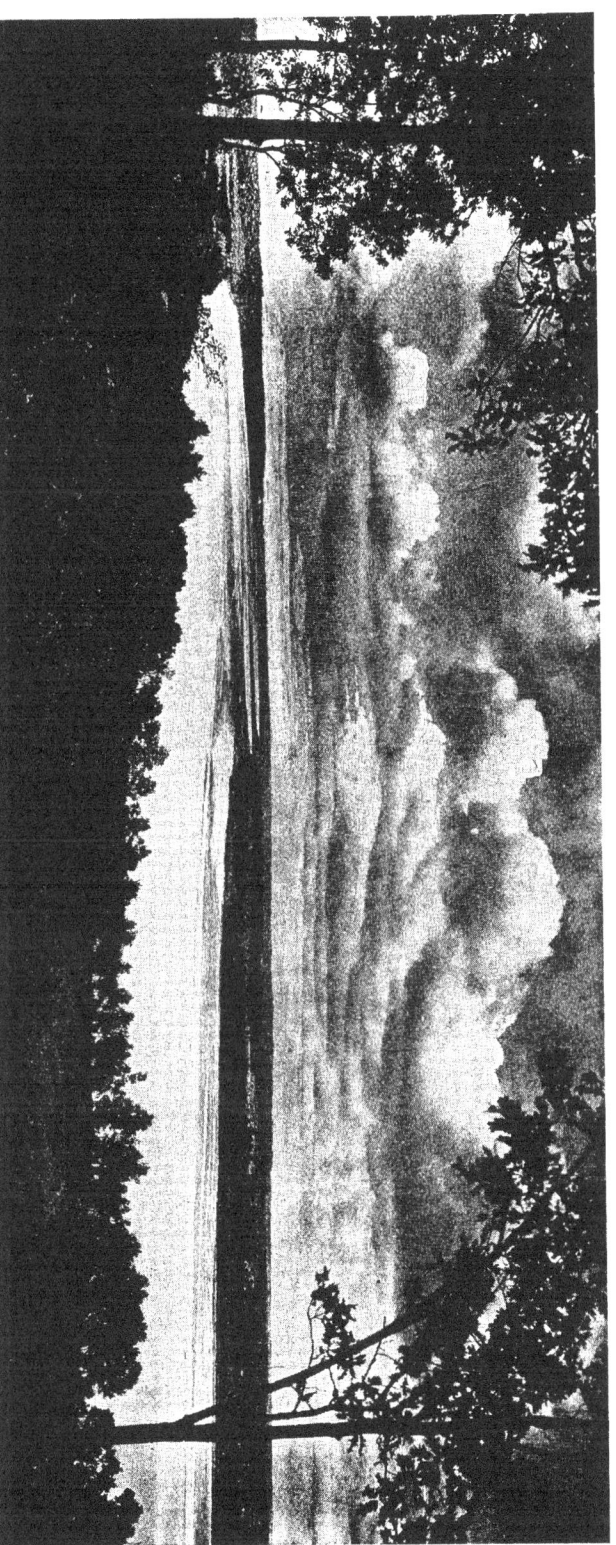

A majestic river flowing through a wide,imposing landscape, is the view one will have from the proposed Thirteenth Street Boulevard at Mandan Park looking northeast.

View from Mandan Park looking northeast.

Missouri River at Sarpy County line looking southeast.
This is one of the many magnificent sights the proposed Thirteenth Street
Boulevard will reveal.

A broad, unspoiled piece of forest-clad land will be between the proposed Thirteenth Street Boulevard and the river.

Vista near Thirteenth and "W" Streets from the proposed Boulevard, showing a ravine in its virgin beauty.

Belt Traffic Ways

INNER BELT TRAFFIC WAY.

The Missouri Pacific Railroad in constructing what is known as the Belt Line, sought a natural route by easy grade around what was then the outer part of the city, and in those early days, little attention was given it. Gradually the residence district developed out to it, and beyond it, until now the railroad route is practically through the middle of the residence section. If the railroad were not already there, it is a question if the city would desire to have it in its present location, but with conditions as they are, we should minimize its objectionable features to the residence district as much as possible, and take advantage of the great service it renders as distributor of materials needed by the city, as a creator of splendid locations for industries and factories.

As a distributor of building materials and coal, this railroad shortens the expensive haul by wagon or truck through the streets, which makes possible a saving in cost of delivery to the consumer. It clears the street of much undesirable traffic, and saves much wear and tear on street pavements. The saving to each citizen individually may be small, but in the aggregate it is immense.

As a creator of industrial sites, it makes possible the location of factories, with good housing facilities close at hand. Needless to say that this is of great importance for the efficient factory of today.

At present the values of real estate in the district along the Belt Line, are low, with about 75 per cent of the land unimproved. It has not been wanted for residence purposes, and it seems to have lacked something for industrial use. Only a little study is necessary to see that what it lacks primarily, is street accessibility. Although there are frequent platted streets, many because of location or steep grades are not suitable for traffic.

The thing needed is a street or traffic way following the same natural route that the railroad follows. This would make a street with an easy grade which nowhere exceeds four per cent, and for the most part, is below three per cent;

in some places hugging up close to the railroad, and in others, leaving a block or more industrial property between it and the railroad. This traffic way will incidentally define and make more fixed, the line of division between the industrial property on one side, and the residence property on the other, thus helping both to develop.

It is interesting to note that without having any idea or suggestion of a continuous Belt Line Street, and in spite of the frequent streets and alleys platted in arbitrary checkerboard fashion, traffic sought this natural route and teamsters cut across private property or along the railroad right-of-way, making use of several short pieces of this proposed route. Later on as it became necessary to build sewers in these districts, the engineer in charge of that work found it necessary to follow this natural route, and then the city acquired short sections of it by condemnation of private property. Several pieces of this sewer right-of-way, which was gotten in a strip about sixty feet wide, are in existence as follows: From Emmett to Maple; from Lake to Fortieth; from Blondo to Seward, and Saddle Creek from about California to Poppleton Avenue on the main line of the Missouri Pacific. The present proposal is to link together these sections and some parts of present streets that fit in, making an Inner Belt Traffic Way twelve miles long. We now have seven and one-half miles of it. The parts yet to be acquired are through low priced property.

Aside from the benefit to the district locally, the general traffic of the city will find this an easy and convenient cut-off across districts now difficult to get through, and thus it will save a great deal of energy and time to the public at large. The whole city will also benefit by having this district opened and developed to produce a much larger share of the city tax revenues.

OUTER BELT TRAFFIC WAY

The outer Belt Line Railroad, (C. & N. W. R. R.) may at some future time, prove to be a valuable asset to the city. Along this railroad there is splendid future possibility for establishing large industries and yards, and now is the time to plan for a Traffic Way along the natural, easy grade route of that railroad. The reason for, and need of the Inner Belt Traffic Way apply as certainly to this Outer Belt, but are not

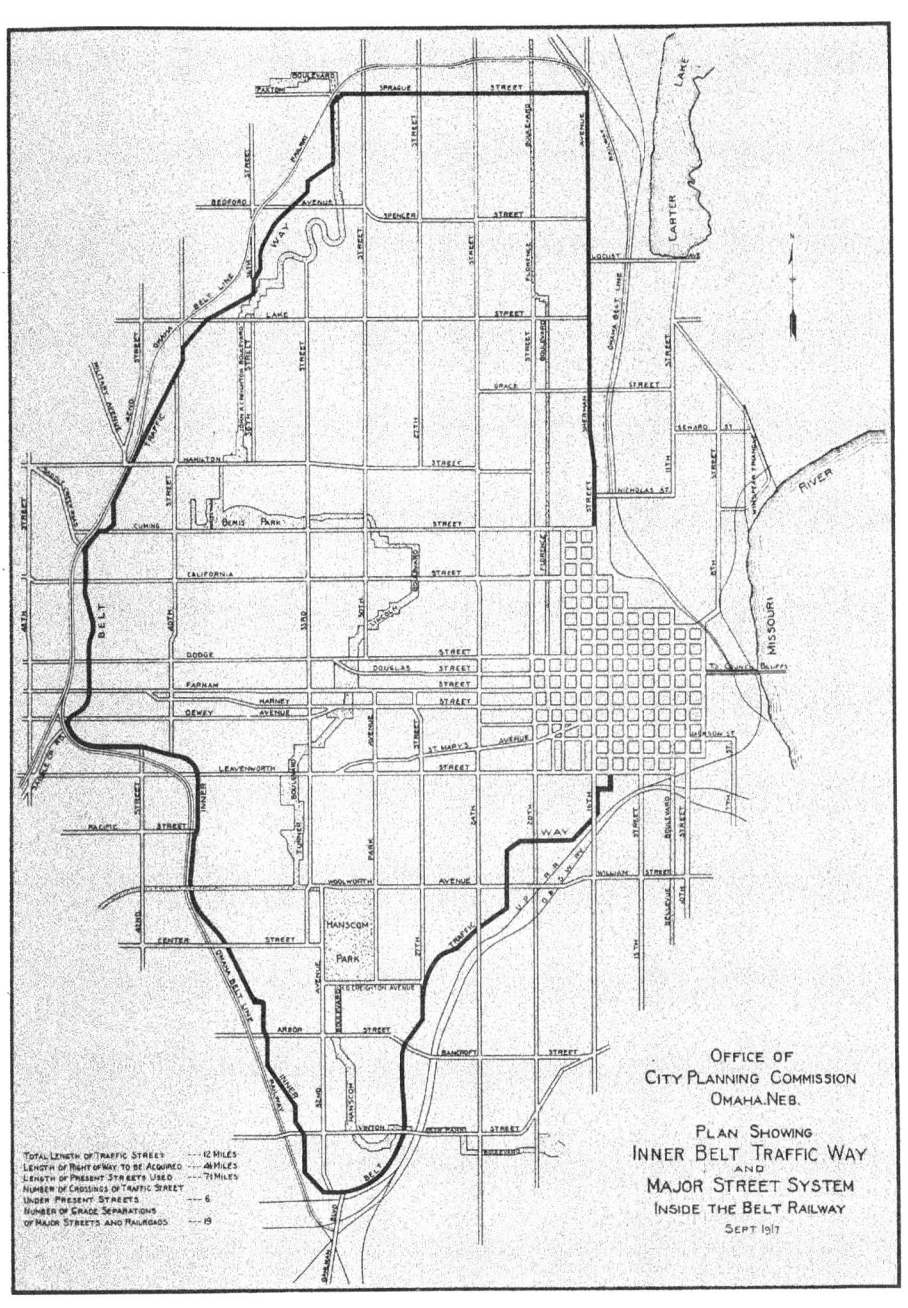

OFFICE OF
CITY PLANNING COMMISSION
OMAHA. NEB.

PLAN SHOWING
INNER BELT TRAFFIC WAY
AND
MAJOR STREET SYSTEM
INSIDE THE BELT RAILWAY
SEPT 1917

TOTAL LENGTH OF TRAFFIC STREET ---- 12 MILES
LENGTH OF RIGHT OF WAY TO BE ACQUIRED ---- 4½ MILES
LENGTH OF PRESENT STREETS USED ---- 7½ MILES
NUMBER OF CROSSINGS OF TRAFFIC STREET
UNDER PRESENT STREETS ---- 6
NUMBER OF GRADE SEPARATIONS
OF MAJOR STREETS AND RAILROADS ---- 19

The movement of vehicular traffic will be greatly benefited by the development of the Inner Belt Traffic Way.

yet as pressing. The indications are that development of this Outer Belt district, once opened up and started, will be rapid. This railroad may be called upon to furnish electric passenger service to a large suburban district.

We have, therefore, planned an Outer Belt Traffic Way, as follows:

Commercial Avenue to be extended north of Ames Avenue, joining Redman Avenue by connecting up various isolated streets, and alleys as shown on the plan. Redman Avenue is then used to Fiftieth Street. From this point, an extension is proposed following the railroad to the north, and to the west of the city, and then southward until intersecting the present Grover Street. This street is then used and connected with Vinton Street by way of a diagonal street. Vinton Street in turn forms the connection with Sixteenth Street, thus completing the loop. This Traffic Way will be practically level in its entire length, except in the south part of town, where the steepest grade hardly will exceed three per cent. It should be of ample width to permit a future widening of the driveway, as the district develops.

Major Streets

The streets of a city divide themselves into two great groups—major and minor. These terms apply, not to their length, nor to their importance in the rounded life of the city, but simply to their traffic value. Thus "minor" streets are streets of relatively little traffic value, being those which have their greatest usefulness in providing a place for quiet residence rather than in facilitating the flow of traffic. These will be considered in a later report.

The term "major" streets, therefore, is to be understood in the following discussion as applying, not as might be supposed, simply to the greater streets of the city; but to the streets of greater traffic importance. While these are usually long and arterial, they may quite often be short or may be only parts of streets. The test is merely that they shall be of especial traffic use. This may be by linking up important thoroughfares, or by providing short cuts for traffic, or by affording channels of such easy grade as to facilitate its movement. In any of these cases, they can be considered as major streets.

Unlike many other cities, Omaha has not had a tendency to take a circular form. This is largely due to topographical conditions, but also in part to annexations north and south. As a result, Omaha has an extreme length compared with its width, and has thus practically eliminated the highly desirable radial thoroughfares.

The railroads entered Omaha and built their lines a long time before the town realized its destiny of becoming a metropolitan city. The railroads follow the natural depressions and thus we have today, the main part of the city and vicinity west, roughly speaking, divided by two eccentric circles touching each other on the east side. Along this point of contact, which is Sixteenth Street, is the intensive business section, extending less intensively around the Inner Belt Line (M. P. Ry.), and with room for future expansion along the Outer Belt Line, (C. & N. W. R. R.). It is evident that should these circular railroad lines perform their functions properly, and be made an asset and a benefit to the city, proper streets should be developed paralleling the railroads as proposed under the heading of "Belt Traffic Ways."

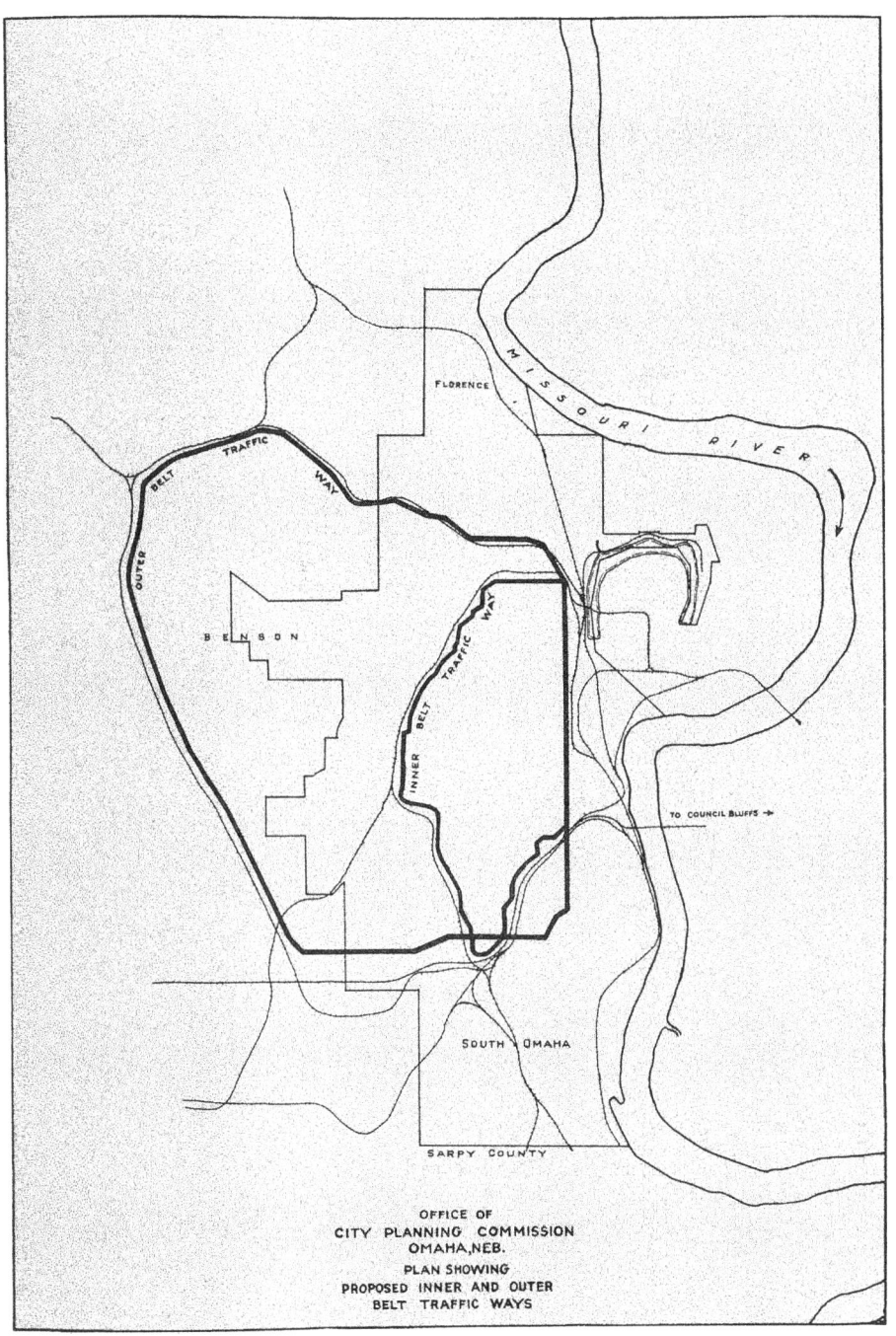

OFFICE OF
CITY PLANNING COMMISSION
OMAHA, NEB.
PLAN SHOWING
PROPOSED INNER AND OUTER
BELT TRAFFIC WAYS

These Belt Traffic Ways, paralleling the railroads, will greatly facilitate the development of industries, and will become basic streets for the future growth of the city.

Intersecting these proposed circular traffic ways, are the major streets north-south and east-west, the Boulevards and the radial streets.

As a general rule, it is not considered imperative to transform all major north-south streets into through streets. The central east-west major streets form a natural division between the north and the south, and to these streets the travel drifts to a large extent. By looking at the proposed City Plan, it will be seen that a number of major streets come from the north and south just far enough to connect with some central east-west streets. The topography of the country, the incorrect laying out of additions, and the expense, make it unpracticable to obtain all through streets.

The City Planning Commission considers it of the utmost importance to work out a fixed plan for the major street system in the suburban district, and have this plan officially recognized in order to avoid indiscriminate platting and the consequences of an occasional lack of foresight. There has been a tendency in Omaha for the subdivider to plat his piece of ground without due regard to the needs of the whole city. A fixed policy in major street planning in the suburbs, will, therefore, be of great economic value to the city when the time comes for actual development.

It is recommended further that the city require those who are using a part of the public street, as far at least, as major streets are concerned, for their own convenience, to remove encroachments at their own expense, thus giving the public the full benefit of the street width.

Such, in brief outline, is the frame-work of the new city plan designed to provide for the future growth of the city, as well as the stability of present values. To realize the ideal of this report, will take a number of years, and considerable money, but it is the opinion of this Commission that the improvements can be affected gradually by following a fixed policy over a period of years. As the development of the city proceeds, however, changes of the plan may be advisable.

North-South Major Streets

SECOND STREET

When the clay banks in the vicinity of Second Street and Dorcas Street have been absorbed in the manufacture of brick, Second Street will be a passable street from Pierce Street to Dorcas Street. A widening is, therefore, recommended between Hickory Street and Woolworth Avenue.

FOURTH STREET

Fourth Street from Pierce Street to Florence Street will be a very useful street when the clay banks mentioned under "Second Street" have been graded down. A slight correction of alignment at Pine Street may be advisable.

SIXTH STREET

Sixth Street between Pierce Street and Bancroft Street, is now quite an important north-south street through a district where good streets are not frequent. The street has a sufficient width and a good grade to meet future demands.

SEVENTH STREET

Seventh Street between Jackson Street and Pierce Street intersects the lower wholesale district, and is considerably used. Being of ample width, it is able to take care of a much greater amount of traffic than that which is now using it. This street, in connection with Sixth Street from Pierce Street to Bancroft Street, offers a good traffic thoroughfare from Jackson Street to Bancroft Street.

EIGHTH STREET

Eighth Street north of Davenport Street, and connected with the latter by a short diagonal street, is now open and in use to Seward Street. From this point, it is proposed to plan an extension north along the railroad yards, connecting with the diagonal street through Winspear Triangle. The usefulness of Eighth Street will then be greatly increased, and give relief to a growing industrial district. It will be also a direct artery to the city-owned Winspear Triangle which has been set aside for municipal docks.

NINTH STREET

Parts of Ninth Street constitute a major street from Fort Street to the proposed diagonal extension of Plant Street in Florence. It will aid the development of the north bottoms and prove to be a useful street. In the central part of the city, Ninth Street has already established itself as a major street. South of Riverview Park and east of the tracks, it may be developed when improvements in this district warrant it. It may be connected with Tenth Street, as shown on the Plan, crossing the railroad tracks at Homer Street.

TENTH STREET

Tenth Street now constitutes the approach from the railroad depots to the business part of the city. It extends south to Hugo Street where it stops abruptly. We recommend that it be connected with Miller Street by way of a curved street about half a block long, and that Mid-City Avenue, which is a continuation of Miller Street, be extended from Twelfth Street to Thirteenth Street, thus giving the district south of Deer Park Boulevard and east of Thirteenth Street, a direct outlet north and south to the major street system. Eventually, a widening may be necessary from D Street to Hugo Street, and along all of Mid-City Avenue.

ELEVENTH STREET

Eleventh Street between Nicholas Street and Avenue "H" (Iowa) is another short street which is much used, and is an important factor in the development of the industrial district north of the Union Pacific Railroad shops. No changes are proposed for this street, except a future extension north to Locust Street.

THIRTEENTH STREET

East of Twenty-fourth Street, Thirteenth Street is the only through north-south street which begins in the central part of the city, and extends south beyond the city limits.

Its width is ninety feet or more from the central part of the city to "Y" Street; from "Y" Street to the city limits it is sixty feet. Should the street car line be extended from Missouri Avenue south, it is recommended that when the developments require it, Thirteenth Street from "Y" Street to the south city limits be widened to ninety feet. The beauty of the river views from this street will increase the volume of travel on it. The grade of the street from "Y" Street south may be slightly changed to advantage in various places.

SIXTEENTH STREET-SHERMAN AVENUE

One of the principal north-south streets in Omaha today, is Sixteenth Street, the north part of which is called Sherman Avenue. Its lack of connections at both ends has a tendency to react against getting the full benefit of it as a thoroughfare. It is recommended that Sixteenth Street be connected at its north end with the extension of Plant Street in Florence, and that the south end be connected with a diagonal street, running in a southeasterly direction west of the German Home, and joining Thirteenth Street. The present width of Sixteenth Street is considered sufficient.

SEVENTEENTH STREET

Seventeenth Street from Leavenworth Street to Grace Street will at some future time, be considerably more used in its entire length than at present, on account of its good grade and its location. The proposed improvement in the grade at St. Mary's Avenue is the only one required.

EIGHTEENTH STREET

No north-south street in the city has probably more travel than Eighteenth Street from the center of the city to Ohio Street. Its abrupt stop at Ohio reduces its efficiency. It is, therefore, recommended to improve the connection to Seventeenth Street, thus getting a through street to Commercial Avenue. A slight correction at this point is required, in order to obtain a direct connection.

The proposed improvement in grade of St. Mary's Avenue and Dodge Street will further establish Eighteenth Street as an important major street.

TWENTIETH STREET

Twentieth Street is now an important street, and if the Dodge Street and St. Mary's Avenue changes of grade are carried out, as proposed, it will unquestionably be much traveled, and will be a very serviceable street for the district between Sixteenth and Twenty-fourth Streets, and from Spring Lake Park to Florence Boulevard, (Ohio Street).

It is suggested that Twentieth Street be widened from Leavenworth Street to Dodge Street, as shown on the tentative plan on file in this office. From Harney Street to Dodge Street, a widening is especially needed because of the presence of double street car tracks. At present the nearest street on the west is Twenty-fourth street, but even with Twenty-second Street opened, as recommended, the block on the west of Twentieth Street will be practically as long as two downtown city blocks. With the widening of Twentieth Street, the opening of Twenty-second and the widening of Twenty-fourth Street as planned, this district will have only half the street facilities of the district east of Twentieth Street.

TWENTY-SECOND STREET

Twenty-second Street from Woolworth Avenue to Howard Street may be made a useful street if opened from Howard Street to Dodge Street. This extension to the north is needed to break the long blocks between Twentieth Street and Twenty-fourth Street. At its south end, it will connect with the proposed Inner Belt Traffic Way, so serving as an outlet for the present and future industries in that vicinity.

TWENTY-FOURTH STREET

Twenty-fourth Street is one of the principal north-south streets of the city, but because of its present inadequate width in places and its abrupt termination at Read Street, much of the traffic from the north, which would otherwise use the street, is forced to find accommodations elsewhere. In connection with Railroad Avenue, it is the natural main thoroughfare for all traffic from the eastern part of Sarpy County going north, and by making a diagonal connection from Read Street to Thirtieth Street in Florence, along the present unplatted valley, a through Twenty-fourth Street is secured. This will prevent a future congestion on Thirtieth Street south of Florence.

It is recommended that Twenty-fourth Street be widened from Pacific Street to Cuming Street, as the present width is insufficient to carry the traffic already there. This widening is one of the most expensive improvements in the contemplated major street plan, but it is justified on the grounds that Twenty-fourth Street will be the principal north-south thoroughfare in the city. Detailed plans and approximate estimates of the cost of the proposed widening, have been prepared, and are on file in the Planning Commission's office. At present, there is no law under which the work can be carried out, without submitting the plan to a vote of the people. The grade crossing at the Belt Line on the north, should be eliminated as shown on the Belt Line plans.

TWENTY-SEVENTH STREET

It is considered advisable to make Twenty-seventh Street from Miller Park to Hamilton Street a major street. This district between Twenty-fourth Street and Thirtieth Street is thickly populated and has a considerable number of dead-end streets. This condition makes it desirable to have a through street intersecting the district which shall connect at its south end with a major east-west street. To accomplish this, it is recommended that Twenty-seventh Street be extended from Bristol to Binney Street, a distance of about a quarter of a mile, and its grade crossing at the Belt Line eliminated. The street needs widening from Spaulding Street to the alley north of Spaulding Street.

From Hamilton Street to Farnam Street, Twenty-seventh Street has partly disappeared. From Farnam Street south to "Sheely," it is a distinct and much used street, and serves as an admirable connection between the Sheely district and the industries along the U. P. R. R. to the central part of the city. A correction at Dewey Avenue should be affected, as shown on the plan.

PARK AVENUE—(Twenty-Ninth Avenue)

Park Avenue is today a major street, with a width sufficient to accommodate the traffic.

THIRTIETH STREET

Thirtieth Street is now used by a great amount of traffic in the northern part of the city, and is a principal inlet from the north. At the same time, it is the only direct connection Florence has with the central part of the city. This connection, however, is very much broken and undefined. Under present conditions, the traffic south congests, or will congest Twenty-fourth Street, Florence Boulevard and Eighteenth Street to an extent which will prove serious in not very many years. It is, therefore, recommended that Thirtieth Street be widened from Yates Street to Parker Street, opened from Parker Street to Seward Street, widened from Seward Street to Indiana Avenue, and opened from Indiana Avenue to Cuming Street, thus making Thirtieth Street a broad through street from the north city limits to the central east-west streets. It is also recommended that the street be widened where the old city limits joined Florence, the street car tracks moved over to the center of the street, and the grade crossing eliminated at the Belt Line. A widening may later be necessary from Farnam Street to Dodge Street where the width now is only thirty-three feet.

THIRTY-SECOND AVENUE

Thirty-second Avenue from Woolworth Avenue to "A" Street, is at the present time, a major street and should be maintained as such. It will in the City Plan, serve an important function, having connection at "A" Street with the proposed Inner Belt Traffic Way, and farther south with the Stock Yard district as Dahlman Boulevard.

DAHLMAN BOULEVARD

Dahlman Boulevard or street as it should be more properly called, is the most logical approach from the north to the Stock Yards, and to the thickly populated district surrounding it. Its connection with "O" Street through the Stock Yards on the south, and with the proposed Inner Belt Traffic Way, makes it a valuable connecting street between two separated parts of the city. It is recommended that a connection be made between Dahlman Boulevard and Thirty-sixth Street just south of the tracks, as shown on the Plan. Where Dahlman Boulevard joins the proposed Inner Belt Traffic Way, a correction should be made at the southwest corner.

THIRTY-THIRD STREET

Between Thirtieth and Fortieth Streets in the central part of the city, there is at the present time no through north-south street. The inconvenience to the people living in this district or doing business there, is apparent. Thirty-third Street from Center Street to John A. Creighton Boulevard, can easily be developed into a major street by an extension of half a block from Maple Street to the Boulevard, and grading from Leavenworth Street to Jackson Street. The street at this point is now open, but the grade prohibits travel. To obtain a satisfactory grade, the Boulevard at the intersection of Jackson Street should be raised slightly. Incidentally, this action will improve the grade of the boulevard.

THIRTY-SIXTH STREET

North of Hamilton Street and south of Center Street it is recommended to develop Thirty-Sixth Street northward and southward as a major street. At Corby Street it will connect with the Inner Belt Traffic Way, and with the boulevard, thus giving the north part of the city and the western part of Florence a direct connection with many of the main streets. Various openings and widenings will have to be made in order to get a through street from Hamilton Street north, running through the western part of Florence and connecting with the paved road to Briggs. An elimination of the grade crossing at the Belt Line and a street viaduct over the Northwestern R. R. tracks at Redman Avenue is recommended. Beginning in Sarpy County to the south, Thirty-sixth Street now extends to Wright Street. An extension to Center Street, paralleling the Belt Line on the west side, and a street viaduct over the Burlington tracks at "I" Street, are recommended. This will give a large territory in the south part of town, and Sarpy County, a through street, connecting with several east-west streets.

FORTIETH STREET

Fortieth Street from Hamilton to Dodge is now considered a main thoroughfare. By making a few minor corrections at various intersections, Fortieth Street can be made a good north-south major street from Redman Avenue to the Inner Belt Traffic Way. North of Leavenworth Street, the grade crossings of the Belt Line at Lake Street may at some future time be eliminated.

FORTY-SECOND STREET

Forty-second Street from Redick Avenue to Military avenue serves a district now under development. At present it stops at Seward Street without giving the traffic a chance for an outlet southward. A one block extension to Military Avenue at the intersection of Charles Street, will provide this. A widening is needed on the east side of the State Mute Institute. Other minor corrections will be required in the same locality.

South of Dodge Street, Forty-second Street has practically established itself as a major street and ought to be maintained as such; a viaduct at "Q" Street across the Burlington tracks and minor corrections and widenings are needed.

FORTY-EIGHTH STREET

Forty-eighth Street is a continuation of a section line road in Sarpy County, and, running straight north to Redick Avenue, is one of the longest north-south streets in the city.

It is recommended that the railroad grade crossing at Leavenworth Street be eliminated; that the street be given a uniform width of at least sixty-six feet, and that all extensions and connections observe the present alignment.

FIFTY-SECOND STREET

Fifty-second street is now an important north-south street from Kansas Avenue to Center Street. At its north end it connects with the proposed Outer Belt Traffic Way. A correction at Leavenworth Street and a few grade changes will make it a major street of great importance. The elimination of the grade crossing at the Belt Line Railway north of Center Street is recommended.

SIXTIETH STREET

South of Leavenworth Street, Sixtieth Street is a well established and considerably used street, connecting with the Sarpy Mills road to Papillion. The grade crossings are eliminated except that of the Missouri Pacific, which should be eliminated at some future time.

The principle laid down in the beginning of this report that all north-south major streets need not be through streets, is here illustrated. The existing conditions in the district from Leavenworth Street to north of Hamilton Street along the line of Sixtieth Street, make it necessary to stop it at Leavenworth Street. Its northern section begins at Blondo Street and extends through Benson and Briggs. This north part of Sixtieth Street is known as the Orphanage Road.

SIXTY-SIXTH STREET

The district between Sixtieth Street and Seventy-second Street, and between Center Street on the South and the Outer Belt Traffic Way on the north, is sadly in need of a north-south major street, which shall conveniently connect with the major east-west streets. On the proposed plan, various pieces of existing streets or roads have been connected up so as to form a fairly continuous street from Center Street to the Outer Belt Traffic Way. As this is an undeveloped district and the topography is rough, the proposed street will fulfill all practical requirements.

SEVENTY-SECOND STREET

Seventy-second Street is the most westerly street in the city, connecting Ralston to the south with Benson and the yet undeveloped district north of the Outer Belt Traffic Way. It is considerably used, extending unbroken north-south for a distance of about nine miles and intersecting all the principal major east-west streets of the city. The width is considered sufficient, but the grade may be improved in places. When the development requires it, the railroad grade crossings should be eliminated.

SEVENTY-EIGHTH STREET

The large undeveloped district west of Seventy-second Street, which at present is outside the city limits, needs a major north-south street. We find in Benson Acres and in Keystone Park, several contour streets which may be made parts of this future major street. It is suggested that the present Seventy-eighth Street be extended north to Dodge

Street, and that it be platted north from the Outer Belt Traffic Way, and to follow the center line of sections 14 and 11. It will then connect with the present contour street in Benson Acres, which under various names, eventually connects with Military Avenue. To carry Seventy-eighth Street through without a break would be impractical and unnecessary.

NINETIETH STREET

Ninetieth Street has been included in the major street plan, as it is a through north-south road from Center Street to Military Avenue. From Military Avenue to Maple Street, it practically parallels the Outer Belt Line on the west side. Having a good grade, it will in the future play an important part in the development of the western part of the city.

NINTH STREET, IOWA

Ninth Street in Iowa belongs rightfully to the Omaha street system in spite of its being located in another state. It is considerably used, especially in the summer, because of the access it furnishes to the Carter Lake Club House, and it is of value in connecting two major east-west streets.

East-West Streets

(Beginning at the extreme north end of the City)

McKINLEY STREET

McKinley Street in the north part of Florence, is a part of the High Road to Blair and of the Briggs road. It is extensively used and gaining importance, because it forms the connecting link between these much traveled county roads and Thirtieth Street, the principal major street leading south from Florence. Its present width of 82.5 feet is considered sufficient, but some improvements are needed at its intersection with Thirtieth Street and the Blair road.

STATE STREET

State Street in Florence, the only long east-west street for some distance, has been included in the major street plan.

It extends from Main or Thirtieth Street west along the north side of Forest Lawn Cemetery to the intersection with the valley road from Benson to Florence.

The grade is not good, but future correction may be worked out as this section of the city develops a greater need of a cross-town street.

POTTER STREET

We recommend that Potter Street in Florence be considered a major street from Thirtieth Street to Thirty-Sixth Street. It is now the main approach to Forest Lawn Cemetery, and has a street car track. When the contour street from Benson to Florence is a reality, Potter Street will form its easterly part, connecting it with the major street system.

PLANT STREET

Plant Street in Florence extends now from the east city limits to Thirtieth Street. A diagonal extension is recommended from the east city limits southeast to Ninth Street, and from Thirtieth Street southwesterly along the valley to Curtis Avenue at the intersection of the boulevard. A curving diagonal street following the contours of the ground is thus obtained, which will be of great advantage to future developments.

REDICK AVENUE

Redick Avenue, when properly developed, will be of great value to the northwestern part of the city, connecting as it does, with all main streets leading in from the north. As portions of Redick Avenue are not now used, care should be taken that when the property is opened, the alignment of the street is preserved.

EAST OMAHA STREET

The maintenance is recommended of a present county road now starting at Ninth Street and Ellison Avenue, and going east along the shore line of Florence Lake. This may be considered a major street, providing an effective outlet for the district.

FORT STREET

Fort Street from Thirtieth Street to Florence Boulevard is now considerably used, and should be maintained as a major street. The topographical conditions make it undesirable to open Fort Street between the boulevard and Sixteenth Street. From Sixteenth Street east, however, Fort Street has been included in the major street plan, with the idea that it be connected eventually with east Locust Street, through the following streets in East Omaha: Thirty-third Street, Avenue L, and Twenty-eighth Street. It would then make a loop through the bottom land around Carter Lake.

AMES AVENUE

Ames Avenue is now a much used route east-west. We propose that when the property west of Fifty-second Street is developed it shall be extended to join Seventy-second Street by way of a contour street as shown on the Plan. A direct connection with Military Avenue is also possible and may be desirable, but will involve heavy grades.

SPRAGUE STREET

Sprague Street from Sixteenth Street to John A. Creighton Boulevard, (Thirty-first Street) is a part of the proposed Inner Belt Traffic Way. To provide a much needed traffic street into the district adjoining the Paxton Boulevard west of the Belt Line, it is recommended that it be extended to Forty-second Street, the west abutment of the present railroad bridge over the Boulevard being rebuilt to accommodate the passage of Sprague Street under the railroad.

BEDFORD AVENUE

The existing Bedford Avenue can be enhanced in value by a short diagonal connection to Spencer Street at Thirtieth Street, and by eliminating the grade crossing at the Belt Line. A major east-west street on a good grade, and with ample width, will then be created from Sixteenth Street to Fifty-second street, intersecting three different boulevards, and the Inner Belt Traffic Way.

LOCUST STREET

Locust Street is now used as a traffic street east of Sixteenth Street, connecting with East Omaha, and the part of Iowa which a change in the course of the river left on the Nebraska side. Its viaduct over the tracks makes it important as the approach to the industrial district, to the pleasure resorts on the lake, and as a connection with the East Omaha bridge across the Missouri River. Some correction is needed near the river bridge.

MAPLE STREET

Maple Street (old main street in Benson) is now a much used country road west of Benson, leading into the city from the west, and connecting with Military Avenue. It is recommended that this part of it be developed as a major street.

LAKE STREET

Lake Street is now one of the principal east-west thoroughfares in the northern part of the city. It extends from Sixteenth Street to Forty-fifth Street on a good grade, and with a sufficient width. In order to make it a still more useful street, an extension is recommended to Forty-eighth Street where it will join Military Avenue. The elimination of the grade crossing at the Belt Line will have to be affected at some future time. At present it is impractical on account of the industries located in the vicinity. From Sixteenth Street to Eleventh Street, Lake Street is not now opened. East from Eleventh Street in the East Omaha industrial district, it is a much used street, paved with cobble stone, and is known as Avenue 'H" through the Iowa territory. It is connected with Eleventh Street, and should connect with the bridge across the river.

BLONDO STREET

Blondo Street from Fifty-second Street west along the south side of the Country Club, and connecting with the county section line road should be considered as a major street. At Fifty-second Street it connects with the proposed Saddle Creek road extension, and when this is opened, its usefulness will be much increased.

GRACE STREET

It is recommended that Grace Street be considered a major street from Twenty-fourth Street east to Eleventh Street, and that a street viaduct be erected over the railroad tracks, beginning at Sixteenth Street and ending west of Eleventh Street. Grace Street will then serve as an outlet for a district with excellent opportunities for industrial development.

SEWARD STREET

Seward Street between Eleventh Street and Eighth Street is now in use. An extension of this street about one block east will make another connection with the city-owned Winspear Triangle, which has been set aside as a site for municipal docks.

HAMILTON STREET

Hamilton Street has large possibilities as a future major east-west street. There is no reason why it cannot extend from Sixteenth Street to a contour street west of the Outer Belt Line, intersecting the Inner and Outer Belt Traffic Ways, the boulevards and all of the principal north-south major streets. The street width and grade are generally good. To make this a through street, some correcting is needed as follows: Connect the present Hamilton Street with Paul Street by making a slight correction and extend Paul Street from Eighteenth Street to Sixteenth Street.

NICHOLAS STREET

Nicholas Street east of Sixteenth Street is now a very important street, carried over the tracks by a viaduct and serving a number of industries and yards in that vicinity. Its connection insures it a permanent place as a major street. No changes are considered necessary.

CUMING STREET

Cuming Street long ago established itself as a major east-west street. It extends from Fifteenth Street to Fifty-second Street, with the grades good to Forty-fifth Avenue, where the proposed Saddle Creek road will provide an outlet for heavy traffic from the northwest. A slight correction is necessary at Fiftieth Street.

CALIFORNIA STREET

California Street, and its extension as Underwood Avenue, is a long through street extending from down town far into the country. Its lack of development west of Fortieth Street is responsible for the comparatively small amount of traffic which uses it. We, therefore, recommend that the grade of California Street be raised at Saddle Creek road; that the grade crossing at the Belt Line be eliminated; that the junction of California Street and Underwood Avenue at Forty-eighth Street be corrected, and that Underwood Avenue be connected at Sixty-ninth Street with a county road which continues west across the Northwestern Railroad and becomes the Dodge Street Road (Lincoln Highway). Considerable grading will have to be done through some of the undeveloped sections, but considering the value which the street will have, both to the city and to the districts which it intersects, the expense will be justified. A widening is recommended and can easily be affected from Forty-fifth Street to Forty-eighth Street.

DODGE STREET

The location of Dodge Street and its connection with the county, make it one of the principal east-west major streets. Betterment of grades between Seventeenth Street and Thirty-first Avenue, are recommended. These were shown on profiles and plans which we sent to the City Council with our recommendations in July of this year.

DOUGLAS STREET

Douglas Street is an important street in the down town business district. We have recommended opening it from Twenty-fourth Street to Twenty-fifth Avenue, correcting its alignment at Twenty-seventh Street, and raising the grade slightly at Twenty-fourth Street. This change will make it a good street to Twenty-ninth Street where the through traffic would divide between Dodge Street and Farnam Street. This opening will especially relieve Farnam Street at Twenty-fourth Street, and will generally help the traffic conditions in the center of the city. It may be found advisable later to reduce the grade of Douglas Street west of Twenty-ninth Street, opening it into Turner Park, and make an angling roadway through Turner Park to Thirty-first Avenue and Dodge Street, thus giving it a more direct connection to the west. West of Turner Park, its continuation is impractical on account of local conditions, until it reappears at Forty-second Street. Its width from the river to Twentieth Street is 100 feet; from Twentieth Street to Twenty-fourth Street 80 feet, except in front of three properties which project beyond the 80 foot line, and narrow the street to 64 and 66 feet. Before any extensive development takes place west of Twentieth Street, Douglas Street should be given a uniform width of 80 feet between Twentieth Street and Twenty-fourth Street.

FARNAM STREET

Farnam Street is one of the best east-west major streets in Omaha. While traffic conditions on the street can hardly be considered congested, there are many times when there are annoying traffic delays. This condition will be relieved by the proposed improvement of the other central east-west streets. Its width will then prove ample to take care of the traffic for a long time to come. A minor correction at the intersection of Happy Hollow Boulevard is suggested, in order to facilitate the flow of the traffic to and from Dodge Street.

HARNEY STREET

The possible importance of Harney Street as a major east-west street, and a relief to the traffic on Farnam Street, cannot be over-estimated. At present its insufficient width in places, and its lack of proper outlet, are consequently a detriment to the whole business district; in fact, to the whole city. It is recommended that Harney Street be widened to 80 feet from Twentieth Street to a point approximately 400 feet west of Thirty-first Street, opened between Thirty-sixth Street and the alley east of Thirty-eighth Street, and connected with Farnam Street west of Forty-first Street. Plans for these improvements were transmitted with our recommendations to the City Council in July of this year. The proposed connection to Dewey Avenue, near Turner Boulevard, will relieve Harney Street at the point where it then narrows down to 66 feet.

DEWEY AVENUE

Dewey Avenue appears now in isolated places west of Twenty-fifth Avenue but does not serve any district satisfactorily. It is recommended that it be treated as a major street from Turner Boulevard to Happy Hollow Boulevard. Dewey Avenue will then provide another needed connection between the fast developing residence district in the western part of the city, and the down-town business district. To accomplish this, the following improvements are recommended: Extend Dewey Avenue east of Thirty-third Street to Harney Street by way of an angling street which will join Harney Street approximately 400 feet west of Thirty-first Street, and open and widen it as necessary from Forty-fifth Street to Fiftieth Street. A minimum width of 60 feet is considered sufficient. The Belt Line will be carried over this street. The extension east of Thirty-third street. connecting with Harney Street has been studied in detail; the plans were made and sent to the City Council in July of this year.

HOWARD STREET

Howard Street from Eighteenth Street to Twenty fourth Street may be considered a major street. A widening is recommended from Twentieth Street to Twenty second Street, and a change of grade from Twentieth Street to a point approximately 210 feet east of Twenty-fourth Street as shown on our detail plan, with recommendation sent to the City Council.

ST. MARY'S AVENUE

As a relieving street to Leavenworth Street, and to the southwest section of the city, St. Mary's Avenue will play an important part, if improved. At the present time it is comparatively unused from Eighteenth Street to Twenty-fourth Street, and only slightly used from Twenty-fourth Street to its termination at Twenty-seventh Street.

A change of grade from Seventeenth Street to Twenty-fourth Avenue is recommended, as is an extension from Twenty-seventh Street to the intersection of Thirty-first Avenue and Leavenworth Street. A minimum width of 66 feet should be maintained. A formal recommendation of this improvement, with the plans, was sent during the year to the City Council.

LEAVENWORTH STREET

Leavenworth Street is now an important east-west major street for street cars as well as for vehicle traffic. Congestion at a few places is increasing, but the improvement of St. Mary's Avenue will relieve this.

It is recommended that the railroad grade crossings at Thirty-ninth Avenue and Forty-eighth Streets be eliminated.

PACIFIC STREET

Pacific Street west of Sixtieth Street constitutes the natural approach for a large district west of the city limits. If developed east of Sixtieth Street by a correction between Fifty-fifth Street and Fifty-second Street by an opening between Fifty-second Street and Fifty-first Street, by a widening between Forty-second Street and the proposed Inner Belt Traffice Way, by a change of grade in places, and by elimination of the grade crossings at both the Inner Belt Line and the main tracks of the M. P. Ry., Pacific Street,—in spite of its heavy grade, will be a very important east-west major street from the rural district into the city, as far as the proposed Iner Belt Traffic Way about Thirty-eighth Street.

PIERCE STREET

It is proposed that Pierce Street from Twenty-second Street to Eighteenth Street shall constitute a part of the Inner Belt Traffic Way; from Second Street to Tenth Street it is considerably used, giving outlet to the district along the river. It should be graded from Eleventh Street to Thirteenth Street, and will then be a good traffic street all the way from Second Street to Sixteenth Street.

WOOLWORTH AVENUE

A direct connection between Woolworth Avenue and William Street, west and east respectively, of the Union Pacific tracks, is proposed. This would mean the erection of a street viaduct beginning at Twenty-first Street and ending at Eighteenth Street, going over Twentieth Street and the Railroad tracks, and an opening between Twenty-Second Street and Twenty-fourth Street. The bridge approach at Eighteenth Street should be connected with William Street by way of a short diagonal street. Great relief will thus be given to a thickly populated section. The street thus created may not be of much value for hauling heavy loads on account of the undesirable grades, but as affording a means of convenient intercourse between two separated parts of the city, the improvement is justified. East of Thirteenth Street, William Street will require a few corrections. It is recommended that traffic be allowed to use the present Woolworth Avenue Boulevard from Thirty-second Avenue to Thirty-third Street in order that it may reach Thirty-third Street.

CENTER STREET

Center Street is one of the principal streets leading into the city and should be further developed. From Forty-fifth Street to the Missouri Pacific Ry., it will be used as a joint traffic street and boulevard, as discussed under the heading of "Boulevards." Along the north line of the Bohemian Cemetery, Center Street will serve as a connecting link between the extended Saddle Creek Road and the proposed traffic street, paralleling the Missouri Pacific to Ralston. The grade in its entire length is very satisfactory. The elimination of the railroad grade crossing east of Sixtieth Street, will have to be considered at some future time.

ED. CREIGHTON AVENUE

Ed. Creighton Avenue extends from Twenty-seventh Street to Thirty-second Avenue, and has value as a major street in affording a connection between the Field Club District and the Inner Belt Traffic Way.

ARBOR STREET

There is great need of a through east-west street south of Hanscom Park. This section of the city, practically divided into three separate parts by railroads, has no adequate means of traveling continually east and west. By connecting up parts of Vinton Street, Bancroft Street and Arbor

Street, and making various extensions and connections, as shown on the plan, a very serviceable east-west major street can be obtained. The improvements contemplated are as follows: Extension of Bancroft Street from Seventeenth Street east half a block to Vinton Street; the raising of the east approach of Bancroft Street bridge, and the elimination of the grade crossing at the Inner Belt Line at Thirty-seventh Street. Between Thirty-eighth Avenue and Forty-second Street, some corrections will be necessary.

VINTON STREET

Vinton Street from Thirteenth Street to Twenty-fourth Street is now a very much used street, of an ample width and an excellent grade. A development of this street east and west, connecting existing streets, offers an opportunity to obtain a very useful east-west major street for a long distance. Beginning at Twenty-fourth Street, going west, a traffic street can be arranged beside the Deer Park Boulevard, and carried over the bridge used now exclusively for boulevard purposes.

West of the bridge, Vinton Street appears again and continues unbroken to Thirty-seventh Street. From this point, it is proposed to make a diagonal connection through yet unplatted property to Grover Street at its intersection with Forty-second Street. Grover Street then extends west where it is a part of the Outer Belt Traffic Way. The grade crossing of Vinton Street and the Belt Line at Thirty-fifth Street should be eliminated by building a street viaduct across the tracks. East of Thirteenth Street, Vinton Street needs to be widened from Thirteenth Street to Twelfth Street and connected with Bancroft Street at Eleventh Street. Then by using Bancroft Street, we have a good street practically to the river.

GROVER STREET

Grover Street from Forty-second Street west, is an existing street and forms the south part of the proposed Outer Belt Traffic Way. To avoid building another viaduct across the Inner Belt Line track, it is recommended that Grover Street be connected at Forty-second Street with Vinton Street by a diagonal street through yet unplatted property.

F STREET

F Street, though given importance by its viaduct over the railroads, is now merely a local street without distinct beginning or ending. If extended east of Hoctor Boulevard to Thirteenth Street, and west of Forty-second Street to connect with an existing county road at Seventy-second Street, it will become an important east-west major street.

L STREET

L Street with its viaducts over the railroads, is one of the most extensively used east-west streets in the southern part of the city. East of Twenty-fourth Street it is called Missouri Avenue and has been dedicated as far as Tenth Street east of the tracks, though on account of the steep bank, it is not used, from Thirteenth Street east of the tracks. As a connection to the east across the tracks, we recommend a continued use of J Street and Twelfth Street. L Street can then be extended ease to serve a future development of the bottom lands.

No recommendation for changes in this street west of Thirteenth Street is made, as the street is considered wide enough to carry the cross-town traffic of this district.

O STREET

O Street from Thirteenth Street to Twenty-seventh Street is the only possibility for an east-west street between L Street and Y Street and should, therefore, be developed. At Twenty-seventh Street it connects with the viaduct leading to the Stock Yards. At Thirteenth Street it might be extended east to give an outlet for the low lands east of the tracks. Its present width is sufficient, and its grade will be satisfactory if some cut can be made at Twentieth Street.

Q STREET

Q Street, carried over the railroads by viaducts, and extending from Twenty-fourth to Ralston, is probably the most used east-west street in the southern part of the city. No change is recommended for this street.

Y STREET

Y Street may be developed without difficuty, into a very serviceable east-west major street. It is at present open from Thirteenth Street to Twenty-third Street, and from Twenty-fifth Street to Fifty-sixth Street. It is recommended that it be opened from Twenty-third Street to Twenty-fifth Street across the railroad, widened from Twenty-seventh Street to Forty-second Street, and from Forty-eighth Street to Fifty-sixth Street, and then connected with Sixtieth Street by a street paralleling C., B. & Q. R. R. At some future time, elimination of the grade crossing of the U. P. and C., B. & Q. railroads will be necessary.

HARRISON STREET

At the extreme southern boundary of the city an excellent opportunity for an east-west major street will be provided by developing Harrison Street from Thirteenth Street to its intersection with the suburban railroad south of Ralston. The present grade crossing of the U. P. R. R. near Railroad Avenue should be eliminated when the development of the district demands it. An arrangement with the Sarpy County authorities may doubtless be reached whereby a widening of the street will be accomplished. The grade can be made very satisfactory.

Diagonal Major Streets

REDMAN AVENUE

By extending Redman Avenue east of Thirty-third Street, using part of the way the present Saratoga Street, and connecting it with Commercial Avenue, we take advantage of one of the finest opportunities for establishing a major angling street leading into the city from the northwest. The extension will require some correction of Saratoga Street, and the condemnation of some property, but considering the value of such a street to the district and to the city at large, this is well worth while.

This street as proposed, will at some future time be the beginning of the Outer Belt Traffic Way, the argument for which is presented under another heading. Redman Avenue proper is continuous to Seventy-second Street where is stops rather abruptly. It is recommended that it be there connected with the Redick Avenue extension, thus securing another through east-west street.

COMMERCIAL AVENUE

There is no street of more interesting possibilities in the north part of Omaha than Commercial Avenue, but its railroad grade crossing, the grade of the street, and its abrupt ending at Ames Avenue, now render it comparatively useless. If extended to Florence Boulevard, and there properly connected to Redman Avenue extension, as shown on the plans, it will provide an admirable direct connection from Sixteenth Street to a great portion of the northwest part of the city. At the same time it will be a link in the future Outer Belt Traffic Way along the Northwestern Railroad. It is recommended that the Commercial Avenue grade crossing of the Belt Line, be eliminated.

CONNECTING STREET BETWEEN FLORENCE AND BENSON

There is a need of a connecting street between Florence and Benson. Two parts of the city, widely separated, may, when the development in the district demand it, easily and at a slight cost, be connected to great advantage to the large undeveloped section in the northwest part of the city.

Beginning at Potter Street and Thirty-sixth Street, a county road running in a southerly direction, is now in existence. An extension of this road following the valley, will eventually connect with Fifty-second Street north of Ames Avenue. A suitable crossing at the Outer Belt Line (N. W. R. R.) will be a part of the future development.

ROAD WEST OF FOREST LAWN CEMETERY

About half a mile west of Florence on the paved road to Briggs, an old established road appears, running in a southwesterly direction through the valleys. As a diagonal cross country road, it is of great importance to this district. At Redick Avenue it connects with the proposed Outer Belt Traffic Way, which on an easy grade, connects with the major street system.

No immediate improvement is recommended for this street, as it is located outside the city limits, and is in a yet undeveloped district.

DIAGONAL STREET FROM KANSAS AVENUE AND SIXTEENTH STREET SOUTH-WESTERLY TO FLORENCE BOULEVARD

The North Bottoms now have only one connection with the city, and that is by way of Sixteenth Street. A great inconvenience is thereby forced on the people living in this district, and the development of the area is retarded. It is recommended that a new street be made to begin at Sixteenth Street and Kansas Avenue, and run in a southwesterly direction to connect with Fort Street at the Boulevard. The bank east of the boulevard will permit a satisfactory grade by following the contours as shown on the plan.

MILITARY AVENUE

Military Avenue is one of the oldest roads leading into the city. Omaha is indeed fortunate to possess such a street. Its grade development is a matter for future consideration, while its width is sufficient to carry a far greater volume of traffic than now uses it. No immediate change is, therefore, recommended, except a readjustment of the viaduct across the Belt Line where Military Avenue converges with Hamilton Street. As soon as any extensive repair is needed on the viaduct, this readjustment should be made.

ROAD FOR DEVELOPMENT OF WINSPEAR TRIANGLE

In connection with the proposed use of the city-owned Winspear Triangle as a landing place for the river boats, with the necessary railroad yards and freight houses; it is suggested to plan another major street connecting Winspear Triangle with the major street system. This will best be affected by a looped street, as shown on the plan, giving the property an outlet at both ends. The exact route of the street will have to be determined when a plan for the municipal docks has been made.

SADDLE CREEK ROAD

The city now owns a right-of-way sixty feet wide from Forty-eighth and Hamilton Street to Fiftieth Street, north of Woolworth Avenue, which was obtained for the purpose of constructing the Saddle Creek sewer. Part of this right-of-way constitutes a portion of the Inner Belt Traffic Way.

It is recommended to extend Saddle Creek road from Forty-eighth and Hamilton Streets in a northwesterly direction along the creek, connecting with Blondo Street at Fifty-second Street; on the south extend the road from Fiftieth Street, north of Woolworth, in a southwesterly direction to the intersection with Center Street, where Fifty-second Street enters from the north, as shown on the plan. Where the road crosses the Belt Line south of Cuming Street and south of Dewey Avenue, railroad bridges with the traffic under the tracks, are recommended.

TRAFFIC STREET TO RALSTON

It should be the policy of the city to provide better accommodations between the rural communities outside of the boundary and the city proper. Ralston and the large district full of possibilities surrounding it, are now very inadequately connected with the proposed major street plan. A development along the Missouri Pacific tracks from Center Street to Ralston, may see its realization in a not too distant future. It is the opinion of the City Planning Commission that a street, with sufficient width to take care of double street car tracks, should be planned from Center Street along the Missouri Pacific Railroad to Ralston, with enough space between the street and the railroad to allow for industrial development. This street, which follows the natural draws, will at the same time, serve as a right-of-way for a principal sewer from Saddle Creek and the Papillion drainage districts. Center Street will constitute the connecting link between this street and the Saddle Creek Road, thus giving the city a continuous diagonal street about eight miles long, in a northeasterly direction from Ralston, intersecting all the principal major streets.

DIAGONAL STREET BETWEEN FORTY-SECOND STREET AND CENTER STREET

The topography of the southwest part of the city is such that there is a great need of thoroughfares following the contours. These will help the development, and when once constructed, will be of material assistance to the people occupying this district. We recommend that a diagonal street be planned from the north end of the Forty-second Street viaduct at west "C" Street, to Center Street about Fifty-sixth Street. For the entire distance, this can follow a natural depression of the ground, furnishing easy access to the cemeteries on Center Street from the west part of old South Omaha, and proving of considerable importance as a traffic street for the industries and yards along Saddle Creek Road. Its connection with the proposed traffic street to Ralston, by way of Center Street, and with a proposed boulevard along Center Street, lends it still more importance. The district through which the proposed diagonal street is planned, is still unplatted. This road through the valley, will save the city a great deal of money in building sewers in that district when they are needed.

CONNECTING STREET BETWEEN ARBOR STREET AND SPRING STREET

West of the Inner Belt Line, in the southwest part of the city, a diagonal connection, beginning about Arbor Street and Thirty-eighth Avenue, and going southwesterly through a valley on easy grades to Spring and Forty-second Streets, as shown on the plan, is recommended. The topography of the country, and the desirability of acquiring a right-of-way for a sewer through this locality, as already proposed by the Engineering Department, justifies the proposed diagonal street. This section is now almost entirely undeveloped.

CONTOUR STREET CONNECTING THIRTEENTH STREET WITH Y STREET

The southeast part of the city between O Street and Y Street, and east of Twentieth Street, is rich in ravines and draws, but has a very inadequate street plan. It is evident that the adoption of the checkerboard plan has been unfortunate for this part of the city. It may prove necessary to vacate many of the present streets, and plan new ones following the contours. These contour streets will, at the same time, give an opportunity for the construction of sewers. As a part of the major street plan, it is proposed to plan a street beginning at Seventeenth and Y Streets, running in a northeasterly direction along the east slope of the ravine, and ending at Thirteenth Street near P Street. Secondary contour streets in this section are contemplated, and will be considered in future reports.

DIAGONAL STREET BETWEEN THIRTY-SIXTH STREET AND FORTY-EIGHTH STREET SOUTH OF L STREET

We suggest that study be authorized for a diagonal street east of the Burlington tracks, paralleling the railroad from Thirty-sixth Street and L Street to the south city limits. An easy grade and cut-off of considerable distance could be secured. Such a street would be a great help to that district, furnishing an outlet for many short dead-end streets. It would add to the value of trackage property, would avoid the necessity of several railroad crossings, and would extend more or less directly from the south county line at about forty-eighth Street to the business district.

CONNECTION BETWEEN SECOND STREET AND SIXTH STREET

It is suggested that Second Street and Sixth Street be connected by a contour street following the north side of the ravine south of Dorcas Street at such time as Second Street is opened.

GIBSON

The part of the city located south of Bancroft Street and between Riverview Park and the river, is commonly called "Gibson." At present it is much isolated on account of its poor connection with the rest of the city. By developing Ridge Avenue, and connecting it at Hascal Street, with an existing contour street leading in a northwesterly direction, and then by extending this contour street to Bancroft Street, an excellent outlet for Gibson may be obtained.

SARPY AVENUE

In the south part of the city, a county road known as "Sarpy Avenue" has established itself as a main traveled street. Its east end connects south of Y Street with Railroad Avenue, which is a continuation of Twenty-fourth Street. This street, with its continuation in Sarpy County, has been included in the major street plan. An elimination of the Union Pacific grade crossing is reserved for future consideration.

HOCTOR BOULEVARD

Hoctor Boulevard would be a very serviceable major street if extended from F Street in a southeasterly direction to intersect with Thirteenth Street, following the east bank of the ravine west of the German Home. A diagonal street like this would be a distinct help for the future development of this district, and would also be useful as a connecting link between Spring Lake Park and the South River Drive, tying the latter into the Inner Boulevard System.

TRAFFIC CENSUS

To determine the amount of traffic carried by each of the east-west central streets, a traffic census was taken during the month of October, 1917. This census disclosed the facts summarized as follows:

CENSUS TAKEN FROM 7:00 A. M. TO 7:00 P. M. 100 FEET EAST OF TWENTY-FOURTH STREET ON THE VARIOUS STREETS

	No. of pleasure cars	No. of trucks	No. of horse-drawn vehicles	No. of street cars	No. of motor cycles	TOTAL
Leavenworth	1740	1035	413	613	152	3953
St. Mary's Ave.	126	33	12		2	173
Howard	380	150	43		12	585
Harney	3072	696	180		81	4029
Farnam	3668	719	127	524	77	5115
Douglas	1124	328	109		31	1592
Dodge	802	171	67	240	34	1314
California	442	176	60		19	697
Cuming	1116	914	456	840	35	3361
Hamilton (Paul)	8	19	72			99

INDEX

To Major Streets and Boulevards

INDEX—(CONTINUED)

CPSIA information can be obtained
at www.ICGtesting.com
Printed in the USA
BVHW041000180119
538188BV00006B/67/P

9 780265 230213